"*Sacred Parenthood* is a transformative guide for parents and caregivers who seek to nurture their children—and themselves—with deep intention and love. Aizaiah and Nereyda Yong offer the SACRED framework—settle, acknowledge, curiosity, restore, enjoy, and dance—as a practical and spiritual road map for parenting as a contemplative, life-giving practice. With wisdom, compassion, and authenticity, they invite us to embrace parenting not just as a responsibility, but as a sacred path of connection, growth, and joy. This book is an essential resource for those longing to cultivate a home filled with presence, grace, and deep spiritual grounding."

TRACI SMITH
Program director for Family Faith Every Day and author of *Faithful Families: Creating Sacred Moments at Home*

"*Sacred Parenthood* is the rare parenting book that knows you are more likely to smell the fragrance of God in the peanut butter and jelly breath of your children than anywhere else. The practices and perspectives in these pages are awash with contemplative wisdom. *Sacred Parenthood* draws upon contemplative wisdom and traditions to highlight the radical possibilities of parenting as a practice intimately connected to the divine vision for peace and justice. Aizaiah and Nereyda Yong have done the impossible—they have written a parenting book that I have finished and that I wholeheartedly recommend."

PAUL SWANSON
Creator and host of *Contemplify* podcast

"Forged in the crucible of the COVID pandemic and lockdown, *Sacred Parenthood* is nothing short of a sacred revolution in its offerings to anyone called to the holy work of parenting. Grounded in the tender fierceness of Love as the Alpha and Omega of all life, Aizaiah and Nereyda Yong have drawn from the transparent well of their own story to provide a uniquely powerful and practical handbook for all who desire to be companioned along their parental journeys. Their spiritually and culturally decolonized approach flips the script on the activation of contemplative spirituality as the basis for deeply authentic engagement with the life of God manifest in relationship with our children.

Every dimension of the SACRED pathway is accessible no matter one's stage or situation of parenting or caregiving. Each story, exercise, or tool has the power to break the burden of caregiving isolation and perfectionism so that ultimately our communities become whole. Whether caring for young children, elders, or the child within, *Sacred Parenthood* will stand out as an exceptionally compassionate and relevant guide for these times and for many years to come."

REV. ANN JEFFERSON
Associate pastor at City of Refuge UCC and director of Community Life and Spiritual Care at the Pacific School of Religion

"This book is just what the world needs right now. At a time when tensions are hot, divisions are growing, and uncertainty is the order of the day, *Sacred Parenting* is a call to reconnect with what matters most: our children, our families, ourselves, and our God. The authors offer gentle wisdom and contemplative practices as antidotes to the high-volume, fast-paced, do-or-die world in which we live."

DAVID M. CSINOS
Associate professor of practical theology at Atlantic School of Theology, founder and president of Faith Forward, research director for Family Faith Every Day, and author of *A Gospel for All Ages*

SACRED PARENTHOOD

SACRED PARENTHOOD

Spiritual Practices for the **HIGHS** *and* **LOWS** *of Parenting*

AIZAIAH G. YONG
NEREYDA YONG

Foreword by Yvette A. Flunder

HERALD PRESS
Harrisonburg, Virginia

Herald Press
PO Box 866, Harrisonburg, Virginia 22803
www.HeraldPress.com

Library of Congress Cataloging-in-Publication Data
Names: Yong, Aizaiah G., author. | Yong, Nereyda, author.
Title: Sacred parenthood : spiritual practices for the highs and lows of parenting / Aizaiah G. Yong and Nereyda Yong.
Description: Harrisonburg, Virginia : Herald Press, 2025. | Includes bibliographical references.
Identifiers: LCCN 2024055131 (print) | LCCN 2024055132 (ebook) | ISBN 9781513815411 (paperback) | ISBN 9781513815428 (hardcover) | ISBN 9781513815435 (ebook)
Subjects: LCSH: Parenting--Religious aspects--Christianity. | Families--Religious life.
Classification: LCC BV4529 .Y66 2025 (print) | LCC BV4529 (ebook) | DDC 248.8/45--dc23/eng/20250214
LC record available at https://lccn.loc.gov/2024055131
LC ebook record available at https://lccn.loc.gov/2024055132

Study guides are available for many Herald Press titles at www.HeraldPress.com.

SACRED PARENTHOOD

Library of Congress Control Number: 2024055131
International Standard Book Number: 978-1-5138-1541-1 (paperback); 978-1-5138-1542-8 (hardcover); 978-1-5138-1543-5 (ebook)
Printed in United States of America
Cover: Artrise / iStock / Getty Images Plus; Ivanova Nataliia / iStock / Getty Images Plus; Olha Furmaniuk / iStock / Getty Images Plus; Tetiana Garkusha / iStock / Getty Images Plus; Olga Shevchenko / iStock / Getty Images Plus; yugoro / iStock / Getty Images Plus

29 28 27 26 25 10 9 8 7 6 5 4 3 2 1

To Amos, Alma, Saúl, and Neddy, who have made our lives possible. May the inheritance we have received from you be multiplied and bear witness to the love that is available to us all.

Whether our homes are happy or troubled, our families functional or dysfunctional, it's the original school of love.

—bell hooks, *All about Love*

Contents

Foreword

In my childhood, the care for children was very different compared to the families of today. Families often lived in proximity to one another and were often members of local churches or shared workplaces. Most nuclear families consisted of the mother and father, along with the auxiliary kinfolk—grandparents, aunts and uncles, godparents, older siblings, and so on.

These realities have shifted as many families have relocated from their families of origin. Our children are often cared for by the internet, television, and cell phones—the babysitters of hard-working parents. Children see their parents early in the morning and late in the evening. If the parents have a long commute, time together is often a meal, TV, and off to bed. Church experiences are often not in the "neighborhood" anymore, and the worship events focused on youth are limited to Sunday, if at all.

This incredible book, *Sacred Parenthood: Spiritual Practices for the Highs and Lows of Parenting*, speaks to today's parents and their supporters who are seeking to care for the family while being a blessing to the time in which we currently live.

Can we "own" our weak places, apologize to our children, and seek help?

Can we lead and learn simultaneously?

Can we be both a friend and a guide . . . a parent to our children?

Scripture says that Abraham was a friend of God. Moses was a friend of God. Disciples were the friends of Jesus. To befriend *and* offer guidance is a lesson in how we are seen, loved, and affirmed by God!

Our children live in a time that they have not yet experienced as adults. We parents and grandparents currently live in a time that we have not experienced as children. We all have so much to learn and to share with one another!

The disciples, the close followers of Jesus, were troubled by the presence of children. I have often wondered how Jesus' followers cared for and about their own children . . . but three of the Gospels suggest that Jesus was troubled when the disciples dismissed the children when he was teaching. In three gospels—Matthew 19:14, Mark 10:14, and Luke 18:16—the same message! "Let the children come to me, and do not stop them," says Jesus, "for it is to such as these that the kingdom of heaven belongs."

In *Sacred Parenthood*, the Gospels speak again! We are invited to share sacred practices that will cover our families in this complicated time. Having Nereyda and Aizaiah Yong and their children as part of our congregation expanded our "worship universe" ethnically and spiritually as they shared a fresh model of family. Their interaction and teaching moments with all the children included holding their attention, authentically honoring their needs and concerns, and encouraging parents to consider new communication approaches. It was and is a powerful reflection of their self-affirmation, and the children and parents were blessed to emulate it.

Because as we cover, teach, affirm and love our children . . . we heal ourselves and our world! Of such is the realm of heaven!

—Rev. Dr. Yvette A. Flunder
Senior pastor of the City of Refuge United Church of Christ in Oakland and presiding bishop of the Fellowship of Affirming Ministries

Preface

This journey began when we found ourselves in the middle of a global pandemic and a radical transformation of our faith. Since the beginning of our marriage, we have dedicated ourselves to learning and growing together. The need for ongoing spiritual development only increased when we became parents. One of the important elements of our training has been in the art and practice of spiritual direction. From our respective spiritual direction training, we have learned the power of contemplative practice is a way to empower and transform our personal lives. We have also witnessed how writing can be a form of contemplative practice that deepens and sustains our lives. We have benefited from the process of putting pen to paper on issues related to trauma, racism, ecological degradation, interreligious education, and, now with this book, parenting and caregiving. Not all writing, however, is meant to be public, so when it came to sharing this book with the world, we wanted to be discerning and intentional. The opportunity for us to launch the Radically Inclusive Parenting Project under the auspices of The Fellowship of Affirming Ministries and the visionary leadership of

Bishop Yvette A. Flunder, inspired us to publicly reflect on our journey as parents and on the practices we have developed to guide our parenthood.

Our hope is that this book will be used adaptively and in community with other parents and caregivers who are committed to holistic liberation. Our greatest desire is that we begin to see parenthood differently and as a viable spiritual path of transformation. While dominant culture often minimizes the importance of our children, parenting, and caregiving, we have experienced God's presence transformatively through parenthood. We see it as deeply sacred work. Parenthood as a viable, spiritual path must be taken up uniquely by each of us—there is no supreme model—and yet it should never be done alone. So, we invite you to take the next step with us by joining God who is already offering healing to all, especially the little children inside each of us.

—Aizaiah & Nereyda Yong

Introduction

In March 2020, we were close to welcoming our third child into our home. Our other children were ages two and four, and we had just moved into a new community six months prior. Because we were new to the area, we had not yet had the opportunity to build tight-knit relationships around us. If that wasn't stressful enough, the Covid-19 pandemic had recently been announced. It felt as though the entire world had turned upside down overnight as communities faced intense shelter-in-place orders. Like many parents in that unprecedented moment, we were suddenly thrust into life at home 24/7 with all our children while also being expected to continue with our full-time commitments to school and work.[1] Needless to say, those days were filled with uncertainty, anxiety, and stress. In retrospect, during this time we were forced to learn that our home life is central to our spiritual formation and that of our children.

The disruption of a global pandemic revealed many surprises, joys, and challenges of parenthood. Parenthood does not look like one thing, nor does it always feel good. As the two of us consider our parenting journey so far, we can identify moments of great anticipation and excitement, but others of great disappointment, regret, and unbearable pain. Even from the moment when we first learned that we were expecting, we felt a sense of overwhelming gratitude and excitement along with feelings of being ill-prepared and terrified to begin a new daunting journey. It is widely known that the birthing process causes the body to go through intense physiological changes. There are new demands, new forms of communication, and new rhythms, all of which make for a wild ride. Partners supporting the one giving birth must practice empathic support, which can only be developed through genuine presence and listening. No matter how one becomes a parent, whether through childbirth, adoption, fostering, or other forms of close caregiving, the changes go far beyond the physical realities of welcoming a new life into the home and family. For parents (as well as kids), the range and fullness of our personal experiences are brought out into the open—whether we want them to be or not! And we learn to face the deepest vulnerabilities of our existence. Our innermost longings, hopes, and desires are bare, and we are thrown head first into the depths of that which is beyond anything we could prepare for.

You, too, might be familiar with the beauty, intensity, frustration, and loss that is part of parenthood. If so, we wrote this with you in mind.

Still, in all the miraculous adventures of parenthood, we have discovered much more about ourselves and the world than we could ever have imagined. We have witnessed how parenthood, one of the most intimate facets of life, can deeply transform us. Just like other sacred paths that the Divine can transform you through, such as marriage or monastic life, we see parenthood as ultimately flowing from the Divine's heart, which is infinitely creative and relational. God is the original source, or parent, from which everything emerges, and our invitation is to remain open and intentional, to know the Divine more deeply, through the practice of parenthood. And that is why we wrote this book, to introduce parenthood as a deeply spiritual commitment that can be thought of as a path of intentionality, sincerity, and openness to God's transformation.

Feminist theologian Elizabeth Johnson talks about God in parental terms, referring to the Divine as the "holy mother of the universe." Thinking of God as a holy mother sharpens our sense of embodied resilience and courage because parenting, too, flows from God's very heart to care for us in our vulnerability.[2] Building off Johnson's image, we are inclined to view the call that many of us have to parenthood as the work of mothering the universe in partnership with the Divine.

While this analogy is one of beauty and strength, it also presumes that much endurance is needed for all that parenthood entails. Many of us might agree that in parenthood, we cannot hide who we are or what is truly going on within us—we are exposed. The real question lies in our response to ourselves and to our children. How do we respond in the joyful moments? How do we respond to the suffering? We have found that we cannot expect to find God only in the high moments—we also find God when we embrace the everyday struggles that sometimes bring us to our wits' end. When the baby can't sleep and cries throughout the night, or when our children spill the cereal bowl (again!), or when our child's attitude triggers something deep inside of us and we absolutely lose any sense of grounding in that moment. We easily feel the weight of responsibility and uncertainty on our shoulders. But none of this means we should cave in to despair—rather, it is from this exact place that we can cultivate our capacity to become alive to the abundance of life in every moment. And in opening ourselves to the abundance of life, we can truly pass along a living and liberative spirituality to our households, a sense of life overflowing into our children that is honest, humble, and hopeful throughout every season of life. We can only give from what we have received, and we pray that we will give from a place of great transformation within.

In our journey as parents, there have been many times when we did not feel that we had much to give at all. We do not believe this is because of our individual faults or lack (although this is the case in some instances), but rather because we are constantly navigating a society that is grounded in oppression and the supremacy of certain bodies over others.[3] For example, in our capitalist culture, we are taught to believe that our worth is tied to our production, or what we do to create profit. We are also taught that Eurocentric cultures are the norm rather than celebrating the beauty of the wisdom that comes from diverse traditions and cultures across the global majority. Because we, as people of color, are surviving these multiple factors, it is easy to just keep pushing and striving. The problem, however, is that we do not take time to acknowledge the inadequacies we feel (based on the messaging from society), and this problem does not simply go away. We go into survival mode, but our survival instincts end up hurting our children and others who are intimately related to us.

As difficult as this is, the good news is that we can learn to channel our feelings into a constructive and life-affirming response by harnessing the wisdom that comes from our experiences rather than rejecting them or putting them aside. We can find consolation in the psalmist, who wrote about the power of waiting upon God to find inner strength: "Wait for the LORD; be strong, and let your heart take courage" (Psalm 27:14a). Waiting is not a passive act. It requires deep confidence and trust in that which is greater than oneself, including one's plans, skills, or powers. As parents, we are invited to wait patiently, hoping and praying for our child's life to achieve its full potential and for all things to be woven together for good. When that potential is realized, there is immense fulfillment and pride. Like the moment when our four-year-old could button his shirt for the first time, and his proud smile filled the room, our hearts beamed with joy. But then there are other circumstances, like when our children experience injury or illness and our anxieties about the future surface. Our first response is to do all we can to improve the situation. But in some cases, we fall short or fail those entrusted to our care. It is precisely these moments of difficulty that either create in us hardened, bitter hearts or mold us into vessels with tenderness and a deeper compassion for the world. The bottom line is that parenthood asks us to become more familiar with the depths of life, from immense hardship to ecstatic joy, offering us an invitation to "taste and see" (Psalm 34:8) the fullness of what life has wrought.

No matter where you are in your parenthood journey, the invitation of this book is to take a journey together. We cannot promise easy or clear-cut solutions, but what we can offer is an invitation to discover a way to live and parent from a deeper and abiding peace. In this spirit, we recognize we cannot go on this journey in isolation. We commit to approaching the dynamic and full range of parenting experiences with care, courage, and community, recognizing that while there is no one model, we can learn a lot from one another and from God.

During this journey there may be moments of connection and warmth; in others, there may be a sense of disconnect or frustration. And that is okay! In fact, it's all part of the process of learning to deeply love ourselves (and others) holistically, the way God does. Our hope is that you can find a way to welcome every experience and that we become aware that we are in this together. Throughout this journey, we hope you will be transformed, but the transformation we speak of is not becoming parents who are without flaws or challenges but rather becoming parents who are empowered with confidence to face whatever may come. We invite you to take a deep breath with us and access openness and curiosity within yourself. Then, we encourage you to find a comfortable place to read in an environment that brings you a sense of grounding. Let's begin this journey together.

The Christian contemplative tradition

We have long wanted resources that would speak to our spiritual, psychological, and emotional experiences and help us cope as parents. During the first two years of the pandemic, both of us began studying more about the Christian contemplative tradition. This tradition reaches back to the earliest Christians who devoted themselves to a personal experience with the Divine through daily spiritual practices. This led them to an awareness of their communion with all of life. There are many examples of Christian contemplatives across all strands of Christianity, including the Orthodox Church, the Catholic Church, and Protestant denominations. While monastic forms of Christianity are often associated with contemplative Christianity, there have been many contemporary efforts to show how contemplation is not something reserved for nuns, monks, religious leaders, or those well studied. It is truly for everyone. For the two of us, it started with those two formative years during the pandemic, when we began to glimpse the connections between our spiritual life, parenting, and social healing.

We have been inspired by numerous individuals from throughout the Christian contemplative tradition (many of whom you will meet in this book). In their diverse perspectives, each of them represents a way of opening oneself to experiencing the Divine personally and allowing that to ripple out into every area of life.[4] A famous scholar of the Christian contemplative tradition, Bernard McGinn, says that the contemplative, or mystical, dimension of Christianity is the "direct and transformative experience of God."[5] In other words, Christianity is most profound and alive in us not as a doctrine to adhere to, but as a personal experience of love that we know intimately and live out of. In the gospel of John, Jesus constantly calls his disciples to move beyond superficiality and to welcome the fullness of experience (John 6:51; 7:37; 15:5). The more we studied the wide and varying contemplative traditions, we found more and more examples of those who offered various ways that we could experience God in the ordinariness of life. As parents this was liberating, because it meant that every encounter with our children carried a potentially enriching discovery of the Divine.

But hold on, you may be thinking. All of this sounds too good to be true—sometimes parenting is just hard! And we totally agree. Divine revelation is not always received through a feel-good process. It appears in the gamut of experiences we all have. What was truly our most radical discovery about the contemplative teachings was not only a newfound experience of God, but how each contemplative bore witness to creative action in the world that renewed and restored what was broken. In our lives, we have seen how the failures we fought to avoid have become some of our greatest teaching moments. Whether it is experiencing a disruption of our plans in a global pandemic, losing a job and having no choice but to relocate, or even being separated from spiritual communities that used to support us—while none of this was easy, we have begun to see how God was working within our lives to foster transformation.

Howard Thurman, a modern Christian contemplative and spiritual advisor to the civil rights movement, frequently discussed the importance of contemplation and social change. As an African American living under constant threat of racial oppression, Thurman taught that the key to understanding Jesus' experience was to view him as an oppressed person who bore witness to the contemplative dimension. Thurman believed that by embracing the contemplative life of Jesus, all those who suffer from oppression can find "a technique of survival."[6] This technique of survival is holistic and includes the intergenerational, material, mental, and spiritual aspects of each person. Thurman's main way of describing this is for each person to come to know themselves as deeply beloved, understood, and cared for by God. Thurman instructed others to listen for the "sound of the genuine" deep within each of us, which is another way of seeing our deepest heart's desires of aliveness and flourishing. For Thurman, life is about learning to devote ourselves more fully to this sound. That is what will bring wholeness. Inspired by Thurman's teachings, we began to recognize the call to parent differently. We felt the need to create space for contemplation and compassion toward all that is suffering within us. As we have slowly learned to do this, we have begun to see our lives change, albeit little by little and in sometimes subtle ways.

Some contemplative teachers provide insight on the power of spirituality that cannot be fully expressed in human thought or language. This is also known as apophatic spirituality. *Apophatic* comes from the Greek words *apo* (away from) and *phasis* (speech). Apophatic theology affirms that God is ultimately beyond any one description. The early church father St. Gregory Nazianzus wrote an untitled hymn describing God as the source of all things, yet that which is also beyond all things.[7] St. Gregory articulates the difficulty in describing this mystery yet affirms that the mystery can be known personally, and that through this knowledge, one finds salvation. For St. Gregory, it is important to be humble before God and mindful that while God can be experienced and known, no one person, description, or experience contains the fullness of God—and therefore, we would be wise to remain open to the adventure and willing to meet God in new ways throughout our lives. This belief is affirmed in Isaiah 55:8-9 where the prophet writes that God's thoughts and ways are beyond any one human way or thought. All of this does not mean that God cannot be known at all—on the contrary, we like to think of this as expressing the truth that there are countless ways to know the Divine personally, and that those ways will continue to evolve because our relationship with God is alive.

In this book, we want to move in an "away-from-speech" perspective and intentionally use many different (and sometimes contradictory) metaphors, words, or symbols to describe God. We will use phrases such as the sacred, the Divine, the mystery, or the ultimate in place of the word "God". While each metaphor may have importance for particular reasons, our hope is that regardless of what words we use to describe God, you realize that God is still not confined to any one moment or description. In addition, our hope is that you, too, will discover and rediscover God in new ways through openness and curiosity.

We have found the idea of God being *alive* in all things yet *beyond* any one thing to be especially powerful as parents because it demonstrates how precious each moment of parenthood is. Although we may look toward the promise of the future or even toward the joy from the past, the invitation to know God is only accepted by living fully in the present. Each moment is unrepeatable. Each day contains a vastness that we can know only if we are courageously open and vulnerable to it. It shows us that our practice of parenthood is a journey, and that encourages us to make space for our parenting to look different with different children or in different seasons.

We have four children. They all require different parenting techniques and strategies to feel supported. Some of our children love to read and engage with the arts, whereas others are more embodied and learn through physicality and kinesthetic movement. It can be disheartening to feel that our desired connection with our children is not landing correctly in a given moment, but the hope is that the Spirit of God is the wisest course-corrector. The word for the Spirit in Greek is *paraclete*, or counselor! Even when our actions do not resonate, we have an invitation to try again, listen again, and be open to a way forward that we could not have predicted. We are describing more than a matter of preference here—we have seen that God is being uniquely revealed through each of our children and all their idiosyncrasies. Understanding God beyond any one construct makes room for the many different kinds of families, households, and contemporary parents.

Our definition of parenthood is expansive. Parenting extends far beyond that of childbearing heterosexual couples and includes foster, adoptive, and surrogacy parents as well as queer parents and parents who were assisted with reproductive technologies.[8] We appreciate how in many Indigenous communities, child-rearing is a communal task and is less focused on the biological parent-child dynamic.[9] We also acknowledge all those parents who have lost children and will forever be parents to those who have now gone on. In all, our intention with this book is to take a both/and approach. We believe that parenting is a sacred practice that can be taken up by biological parents and also by so many other diverse people. Therefore, while we wrote this book based on our own experiences as biological parents, we hope the stories and practices we share will be contextualized and adapted by all who play caregiving roles for children. There is truly no one model for all, and we must all learn to walk our own paths and build the way together.

Contemplative parenting

On the surface, contemplation sounds like a passive activity, perhaps involving a dark, quiet room and alone time. All that may help, but even those factors do not always lead to contemplation. And they may not be possible for parents who are busy keeping their children alive and tended to while living in a household where space or time is tight. Really contemplation is what happens when we become more lovingly engaged with the reality of our own lives. Yes, contemplation involves dedicated practice, but it is less about a specific approach or context and more about cultivating a way of being in the day-to-day that is deeply personal and can take on many forms, such as reading poetry, listening to music that grounds us, or taking time to pause and breathe. Contemplation is radical. It seeks to live out each moment from the core of oneself—to be present, accepting, curious, courageous, and compassionate. When we engage in contemplation, we become empowered by love rather than fear or hate. Contemplative parenting is about going deeper into the love present within our own lives and embracing the journey along the way. It is about being present and available for the here and now, being open to encounter the sacred in previously unforeseen ways. And it has immense implications for creating a more just world beginning where it matters most—at home.

While both of our families who raised us were very loving, neither of us were prepared with actual practices and tools that could support contemplative parenting. To make matters more complicated, our partnership is intercultural (Aizaiah is a second-generation Chinese Malaysian Mexican American and Neddy is a third-generation Mexican American). We did not know it when we first met, but there were many cultural assumptions hidden under the surface of our relationship that we bumped up against when we became parents. Although both of us were raised in close proximity to immigrant experiences, we each received different implicit messages about parenting and how to interact with children.

Perhaps your journey into parenthood also comes with many inherited behaviors. Our invitation is to become more critically aware of what those inherited behaviors are and why they exist within us. By approaching our stories with compassion, we begin to see there are more options available on how we parent. When we became parents, we quickly saw that neither of the models we inherited would be sufficient. Through a lot of intentionality and animated conversations, we have found a path that honors the contours of our experiences and harmonizes it with contemplative wisdom.

Very few of the contemplatives we have encountered discuss parenting specifically. Still, we saw how the principles of their teachings could be reimagined and applied to create deeper support at home. Like every good millennial, we googled contemporary spiritual resources on contemplative Christianity and parenting young children. The results were scant. And none of them considered the experiences of people of color or immigrants. This scarcity cultivated a desire within us to create spiritual resources that were relevant to our family's context and could be supportive to other spiritual, intercultural, and socially conscious households. We have found that parenting from a place of deep and loving connection—what we call contemplative parenting—can change everything. Contemplative parenting created new opportunities for us to learn from everyone in our household. We realized that our children were also spiritual guides and teachers. They have taught us about joy, play, curiosity, anger, imagination, and so much more.

As clergy ourselves, ordained in a tradition that takes social change very seriously, we began to identify connections between the way we treat our children and how we choose to pursue systemic transformation across society. Our own children, our world, needed us to become parents committed to tending to our own vulnerabilities with care. We came to realize that we never really "grow up" in the sense of leaving behind all our past experiences. Instead, we carry each and every stage of our journeys with us—the "little ones" within. Contemplative parenting seeks to become more compassionate towards each version of ourselves longing for connection with us now. If we can do this, we will find that we can also unlearn internalized oppressions stemming from racism, classism, xenophobia, patriarchy, ableism, and much more. By taking a contemplative approach to parenting, we began to understand our work as intimately connected to shalom, the divine vision for peace and justice. We began to wonder, could the liberation we long for the most be most readily practiced in our parenting, right at home?

In the Bible, Jesus teaches that only those who "become like a child" will enter the kin-dom of heaven.[10] As we have grown in our practice and parenting, we have found that this passage reveals the preciousness of all our lives in their most vulnerable aspects. While society teaches us to discard or dismiss these intimate aspects of our experience or view them as "immature" or "incapable," Jesus invites us to see them anew with deep regard. Some of Jesus' most profound miracles involved the relationship between parent and children, such as the healing of Jairus's daughter in Luke 8 when Jesus tells the father, "Do not be afraid. Only believe, and she will be saved."[11] Stories like these demonstrate how parenthood includes the most primordial and sacred aspects of life. Jesus repeatedly said to his disciples, "Let the children come." We extend this same invitation to all kinds of parents and caregivers to journey with us and reconsider how we might participate with the Divine in the sacred call and gift of parenthood. If we are open to it, we can see the sacred path of parenting as a continuous invitation to learn from and with our children about what it means to "become like a child" again. We know that with God's help, we can connect to those tender places within that most long to be transformed.

Engaging sacred parenthood

In this book, we'll share various stories about parenting along with contemporary findings from across the social sciences that help illuminate the importance of parenting differently. We will reflect on what parenting would look like if we saw it as a deeply transformative spiritual path. We call our practice "sacred parenthood" because it speaks to the heart of what we are trying to do: to recognize that parenthood is deeply spiritual and involves our whole selves rather than only parts of us. We see parenthood as an opportunity to become more dedicated to God. Sacred parenthood is not just about living with devotion to God but about more fully living and experiencing our humanity. Parenthood contains so much of our humanity, and that is not to be rejected or excluded. Sacred parenthood, then, is not a happy-go-lucky experience but a deeply holistic and integrative spiritual path.

In this book, we will introduce you to our contemplative parenting practice. It embodies six movements, summed up in the acronym SACRED: settling, acknowledging, being curious, restoring, enjoying, and dancing. SACRED is embodied and holistic. Its six movements are intended to invite you to culturally honoring, collaborative, contemplative parenting that is inspired by intentional connection to the Divine, yourself, and the wider world. It invites creativity, is accessible for diverse cultural contexts, and is flexible to each household's needs. While it can be practiced individually, we hope that you will practice it alongside others and deepen it through conversation and engagement with others—including your children. Both of us have learned so much from the contemplative teachers and practices, which have inspired us to take contemplation to new creative directions. We hope you will feel encouraged and inspired to forge new paths in the adventure of parenthood.

This book was written from our context as the parents of four children, currently ages nine and under. While we can only imagine what the future will bring for our family, we are hopeful that the seeds we are planting today will bear good fruit as our children—and we as their parents—continue to grow. In that, we hope that sacred parenting can blossom in your own family, whether you are in the midst of planning naptimes, navigating the teen years, or even grandparenting. We pray that the ideas we offer throughout the book, to engage each SACRED practice, inspire in you other ways to experience loving, mindful parenting. We have included a list of go-to phrases that we use in the hopes that they will help you at home. Though each moment isn't always easy, with the right practices and the support of community, we can learn to respond to our children from a place of connection rather than judgment.

As we named earlier, the major conviction of this book is that parenting is not just a role we perform, but a sacred spiritual path of transformation. As with any other sacred, spiritual path (for example, monasticism, marriage, or becoming a clergyperson), we believe our response to the sacred path of parenthood ripples out into the broader world. We have written this book to provide concrete practices that you can use as you parent. We know that freedom comes when we realize that God is not to be found in any one way or one practice but in the truth that God continues to guide us in whatever may come. While we continue to discover growing edges about the practice of parenthood every day, it is our desire to share some of the invaluable lessons we have acquired so they can be experienced in your life too. Our children have taught us so much, and our prayer is that you find new ways of relating to those miraculous lives around you with a bit more tenderness. In so doing, may you also experience firsthand the feeling of being known and held in the embrace of God. May this book be of benefit to all parents and caregivers who are looking for practical and spiritual ways to transform their parenting or caregiving so that we help create a world where *all* people experience their own deep preciousness.

1

SACRED Parenthood

Let the children come to me, and do not stop them, for it is to such as these that the kingdom of heaven belongs.
—Matthew 19:14

If you are anything like us, you may have found that resources on parenting usually speak to the psychology of parenting (which is valuable!) but have little to say about the spirituality of it. They also often fail to be relevant to those from diverse cultures and experiences. As people who come from immigrant households, we have often felt that we needed to create the path we longed for by ourselves. In immigrant communities of color, parenting is usually not a solo effort but it requires the whole tribe. Our wisdom tends to be shared in stories and songs rather than doctrines to confess or to-do manuals. Communities of the global majority want to live our way into transformation rather than just thinking our way towards it. We have sought to integrate these cultural sensibilities into our way of parenting too. For example, we invite story, play, food, and song into the ways we can connect with our children and experience mutual learning and receiving from one another as a result.

Although there have been many moments which felt isolating and disconnecting, we are grateful to have met many wonderful human beings from across cultures and traditions who have reminded us about the importance of parenting in connection to our spirituality. In this chapter, we want to introduce you to a practice you can use and apply creatively in your own life. This chapter provides a high-level overview of the six movements of the SACRED practice that we'll explore throughout the rest of the book. After this overview, we'll describe a few key spiritual assumptions that underlie our approach to contemplative parenting.

We are confident that if you are reading this book, God is already at work in you to equip and empower you toward living out contemplative parenting. So, we invite you to take a deep breath and remind yourself of the great Spirit who is at work within and around us, inviting us to trust in the process.

SACRED practice

The SACRED practice is designed to help us become more deeply aware of what we are truly experiencing in joyous as well as challenging moments. Through this practice, we can feel more connected to ourselves and to God (or any other sacred source). With regular practice, we can grow in our discernment to choose a life that feels more connected to purpose and fulfillment for the flourishing of all, especially our children. It is important to note that we do not see this practice as linear or as something all people should emulate in any specific order. As we have been made keenly aware, a major key to the contemplative life is learning to make it personal and not follow a predetermined path. But we hope the SACRED practice is a helpful starting point to begin infusing your parenthood with spiritual wisdom.

The SACRED practice unfolds across six movements: settling, acknowledging, being curious, restoring, enjoying, and dancing. *Settling* engages the importance of identifying practices that foster a sense of safety for us. For many of us, this means retrieving ancestral and cultural practices that have been demonized by colonialism under the guise of Christianity. In this movement, we explore teachings that insist all life is sacred, set sacred intentions for our daily lives, welcome the Divine more consciously into our experiences through icons or other sacred objects, and anchor ourselves in our breathing.

Acknowledging is about noticing what is present in our minds and bodies and working not to judge it (especially our areas of difficulty). We can develop habits that help us connect to a more grounded sense of self while naming what is coming up for us in our experience. When we learn to hold a nonjudgmental posture toward our thoughts and feelings, we can truly learn from them and integrate the wisdom they hold.

As we venture deeper into contemplative awareness, we open ourselves to new insights and understandings. Through compassionate *curiosity*, we can learn to welcome layers of our experience we may have previously missed or disregarded. For example, when we are open to discovering what parts of us are activated by various scenarios or situations, we often discover that underlying thought patterns, familial narratives, or the impact of past experiences are what drive our actions today. A posture of compassionate curiosity can help us hold every part of ourselves, even the most vulnerable, without judgment and in love. This is the idea of radical inner belonging, where we seek to fully embrace our whole selves. As we become more curious, we also engage the power of *unknowing*—asking genuine questions that can lead to greater understanding of what may be needed and gaining insights into the relational nature of love.

In the fourth step of the SACRED practice, we'll share about a transformational way of parenting that fosters *restoration* and overcomes individualism through deep care, reciprocity, and genuine inner freedom. In this movement, we allow ourselves to embrace the lifelong journey of parenthood and the importance of taking accountability for our actions and recommitting to a life of "no harm." As parents and caregivers, we are entrusted to guide the development of our children. The first step toward repairing harm we have intentionally or unintentionally committed is being able to admit our mistakes so that we can change our behavior. Ultimately, this dimension of SACRED parenting is about promoting the restoration of right relationships, which can only be performed through courage, conviction, and compassion.

When we develop new ways to respond to life's circumstances, we experience invitations to soak in and savor newfound connections. *Enjoyment* does not always mean that things feel good or are positive. Instead, enjoyment suggests that there may be a deeper gladness in our lives that is not ultimately about things always going the way we desire. Enjoyment is about the many ways we can learn to appreciate the fullness of our experiences. By opening up to them more fully, we grow in wisdom and connection with ourselves and others. Thus, the more we cultivate compassion within, the more that joy becomes a way of life and spreads outward to others. Compassion then overflows into all our relationships and nourishes holistic flourishing. So, although a life of radiating compassion is not always a mountaintop-like experience, it solidifies and deepens through the small moments in our days.

The final movement in the SACRED practice is *dance*. Dancing is one of the most original and longstanding spiritual practices from across cultural and spiritual traditions. In this step, we talk about embracing the freedom of life and how this includes a call to spontaneity and celebration. Celebration is not just an idea but a lifestyle of gratitude and generosity. The dominant culture so often speaks to our deficits and lack, but dancing is an embodied expression of wholeness.[1] In this step, we talk about different ways of dancing, which is not reserved for the (temporarily) able-bodied. Wholeness for us is connected to holiness, and this can be realized through a call to dance together with all of life, celebrating the gift we have each been given. As we dance, we begin to see how the celebration reflects the new thing that God is always doing (Isaiah 43:19), which invites us to expand our gratitude for the love that permeates all of life.

In the chapters that follow, you'll find a specific practice that we've designed that invites you to live into each of these six SACRED movements. We intend these to be a starting place. As you feel led, we invite you to creatively adapt the practice in a way that best supports you. We've also included ideas for ways to help your children engage in the spirit of these movements. Remember, the heart of contemplative parenting is about being present in the here and now, open and available for the sacred to be encountered in previously unforeseen ways. We encourage you to engage in these practices alone, with your children, and in your broader community. The journey of sacred parenthood is not meant to be done in silos while we carry the burden by ourselves. Sacred parenthood calls us into deep relationships with others who can support us and lift us up along the way.

Beloved

Three key understandings underline our thinking on sacred parenthood and the SACRED practice: belovedness, creativity, and wholeness. First, we recognize that all life is inherently precious to God, because we were created out of an original belovedness rather than original sin. When we as parents can see ourselves as inherently beloved, then we are more inclined to see the inherent belovedness of our children. Genesis 1:31 first introduces the idea of original belovedness: God created all things that were "good" and after creating humanity, God saw that it was "very good." Sin gets introduced *after* the original goodness, or belovedness, which was present in chapter one. In Acts 17:28, the apostle Paul preaches to non-Christians about how it is only through the power of God that each being is able to move and experience blessedness. Paul references the Greek poet Aratus, who claimed that all life originated in, and was sustained through, divine action. Paul rearticulates this philosophical claim to promote the message that it is through the goodness of God that all life is made possible and each is sustained. Both passages of scripture affirm that we are each infinitely loved by a God who created us in God's own image and that our greatest longing is to grow in a personal experience of belovedness, and to share it with others.

Theologian Wendy Farley explores how Christian contemplatives across history have shown our relationship with God to be ultimately about cultivating a greater loving connection. "Contemplative prayer is about *eros*," she shared in a recent interview. She goes on to describe eros as, "A longing for the Divine beloved and a falling in love with the Divine beloved." For Farley, connecting to prayer as contemplative moves us away from judgement toward mercy. In her words, "[Christian contemplatives] do not talk about sin and punishment and they do not talk about God's judgment of us. They talk about how precious we are."[2] When it comes to parenthood, the goal is not to become a perfect parent (although we attempt to do as little harm as possible). Instead, parenthood is a call to return to how deeply we are loved time and time again. Of course, this means that there will be times when we need to apologize, make repairs, ask for forgiveness, or accept that some things will be left unfinished. But whatever comes, we can return to our core experience as beloved.

Creative

As parents and contemplatives, we have come to see life as richly creative. One of the most powerful verses in the Scriptures about this principle comes from Genesis 1:28. The first blessing and command to humanity is to "be fruitful and multiply." Because God is creative, life reflects creativity and is most fully realized through creative action. Life's purpose is to move in creative ways, promoting new life along the way. For us, the call to sacred parenthood flows from both an original belovedness and a creative impulse that we are invited to participate in personally. We have each received this creative blessedness from God, and it is a great privilege to pass this on to others.

Life is not only creative but also emergent. In other words, life is always being remade. It continually offers new possibilities that we could not have foreseen or planned for. The emergence of life does not mean that things are either completely random or predetermined. True creativity lives in the space where the past, present, and future are all interwoven. Therefore, we resist actions that are pure chaos or those that are separated into predetermined outcomes. The wisdom of parenthood flows from an openness to respond to what was, is, and will come. Life gives the option of choice: we are free to choose and to be chosen freely. Genuine love requires consent, and this cannot be bypassed, not even by God.

In parenthood, embracing the emergence of life means embracing a growth-oriented mindset. We learn to see that every encounter has a lot to teach us. Emergence means that there will inevitably be opportunities to practice new ways of being parents and many chances to witness our children transform again and again. The reality is that everything at some point or another will pass away. Whether it is the greatest highlights of our parenting journeys or the lowest moments when we feel completely defeated, nothing lasts forever. We can learn to engage each moment and cherish the whole experience, for it is unique and, like everything else, will come to a conclusion.

Whole

Both of us are ordained ministers in the Christian Church (Disciples of Christ), whose slogan is "A movement for wholeness in a fragmented world." In the earliest stages of the Disciples movement, the major emphasis was on Christian unity. The tradition sought out unity through a weekly practice of the Eucharist, or the Lord's Supper, which is open and available for all people in and beyond the church who desire to partake. One of the more radical views of the Disciples was that laity could administer the communion sacrament, not just the pastor. According to the Disciples tradition, wholeness was all about radical inclusion amid the rich diversity of life. All could gather at the table, and the Lord's grace was expansive enough to cover all.

While the early Disciples often thought about wholeness as unity, their idea of unity was never about homogeneity but about how diverse people and congregations could find covenantal relationship. Hence, as part of the Disciples' tradition, we see *wholeness* as more of a verb than a noun and a way of practicing relational connection. Wholeness is not about a particular transcendent state of being that can be fully possessed by any one person, nor is it an experience without earthly problems. It is a continuous practice of relating to the whole of life through receptivity and love. As Christians, we trust that the Holy Spirit guides us into wholeness, but we also recognize that wholeness may be practiced by those beyond the confines of institutional Christianity. As the scripture attests in John 3:8, "The wind blows where it chooses. . . ." In our own lives, we have learned a lot about wholeness from cultural and spiritual wisdom beyond Christianity. This has been vital for us because any supposed wholeness that is understood as exclusion to others—whether by religion, race, gender, sexuality, or any other category—is no wholeness at all.

To be clear, our position is not relativism (the belief that "anything goes"). Rather, our desire is to promote an openness within Christians to be open to the Spirit's leading wherever and whenever it may be found. Ultimately, the leading of the Spirit is not about converting others to participate in particular cultural practices but about the movement toward deep communion with all of life.

Wholeness is not about making things easier, happier, more convenient, or absent of problems. While the dominant cultures of today promise a life without stress, worry, or chaos, the truth is that a practice of wholeness must learn how to make peace with stress, worry, and chaos. Wholeness is about accepting and relating to the whole of life without exception. Put another way, wholeness is about our capacity to welcome all aspects of life and to do so empowered by the Divine, whose intent is for all of life to flourish. By making wholeness a central spiritual practice we make ourselves available for life to appear to us as it is. It is only then that we can extend compassion, curiosity, and courage in each moment so that life can continuously be transformed. Of course, this is easier said than done, but it is something that we can grow in through intentional effort, supportive community, and divine guidance.

Belovedness, creativity, and wholeness are foundational to all the practices we will share in the rest of this book. We encourage you to draw inspiration from these key ideas as you consider the SACRED practice and make it your own.

At the heart of our spiritual vision is trust that the sacred is always near and available to work through, in, and beyond us. We realize how challenging life can feel at times, especially for those whom systemic forces oppress and impose unnatural rhythms. But we are inspired by the lineage of mystics and revolutionaries who have tapped into spirituality as a resource of strength and courage. They have shown us that is the only way to live fully and well, in the midst of difficulty, and for that difficulty to even bring forth new life.

2

Settle

"Be still, and know. . . ."
—Psalm 46:10

The thought has crossed our minds too often: "I just do not have enough time!" Or "How is it ______ (fill in the blank with any day of the week or month of the year) already?" We live in a society that overvalues speed, efficiency, production, and achievements. Our norm is something we call "grind culture," and its effects are debilitating. In her book *Rest Is Resistance*, poet and theologian Tricia Hersey writes that grind culture "has made us all machines, willing and ready to donate our lives to a capitalist system that thrives by placing profits over people." Grind culture, she says, "weakens our love of self and community."[1] Hersey illuminates the many ills that come from our addiction to the grind. Rush culture brings poor physical health, high blood pressure, and unrelenting stress, and at the root is a belief that something is missing and that we are not enough. We have bought the lie that our lives are only worthy of care if they "produce." Under this falsity, we give our all to achieve the next level, overcome an obstacle, or change the problem, thinking that when we do, there will be peace inside.

Even worse is how these machine-like rhythms rob us of truly experiencing the fullness of each moment. How often do we miss the simple gift of simply being alive? We have been trained to work hard, believing that our sacrifice will bring a greater tomorrow, when in fact we only end up missing the gift of today. When we see goodness only in tomorrow, we never get to actually *experience* and taste the goodness of here and now. Ephesians 3:18–19 records one of the apostle Paul's prayers for the church to know this truth each day: "I pray that you may have the power to comprehend, with all the saints, what is the breadth and length and height and depth, and to know the love of Christ that surpasses knowledge, so that you may be filled with all the fullness of God." In other words, the expansive love of Christ is offered to us regardless of whether we feel we deserve it. Is this not the true meaning of grace?

When it comes to parenthood, we have found that sacrificing today to grind culture never leads to fulfillment. We cause unnecessary stress on our children and miss out on the love that is available to us right now. Psychologist Lauren Cook states that one of the biggest reasons we are seeing a spike in anxiety in children today is due to something called "hurried child syndrome." This term describes how societal pressures to succeed compel parents to put their children in situations that exceed their developmental capacities. "In other words," writes Cook, "we're scheduling them like mini-adults without building in time for their relaxation, play, and dare I say, even boredom."[2] All of this creates a vicious cycle where our spiritual and mental health is compromised, and we suffer. Why is it that in North America, the average person reports high anxiety, isolation, and a lack of well-being? Perhaps we are missing the beauty that is hiding right in front of us, within us, and is available to us always.

The good news is that we can practice something different. In our home, we love watching nature-based documentaries with our children. We are amazed by the beauty of different geographies, up-close explorations into the lives of animals large and small, and panoramic images and sounds that express the grandeur of life. When we reflect on how dolphins communicate through echolocation or how plants communicate through fungi, we are deeply moved to realize the wonder of life. We discover how our lives, too, are connected to this expansive world and the links that tie everything together. You may or may not enjoy nature-based documentaries, but you probably agree that this world has some beautiful scenery. But when our lives are driven by the rush of grind culture and we perpetuate the status quo, it is like we are watching one of those vivid and wondrous films at 5x speed, missing out on the beauty of it all! It is like we are skipping over the beauty of what is right in front of us. But what if we could find ways of slowing things down so we could live the fullness of our lives we have been granted?

Intentional stillness

As an intercultural couple who both come from immigrant families and intergenerational poverty, the two of us found that we had internalized a lot of survival patterns that often resulted in a restless "go, go, go" state with little opportunity to find grounding. Much of this stems from the experiences of our ancestors who were expected to work long hours and meet high standards, without flaw, to ensure employment security and safety because their families' survival literally depended on it. Especially knowing this, we honor our ancestors who did not have the same luxury to practice settling, or stillness, because they were busy surviving the harsh realities of oppression and violence. Still, we realized early on in our parenting that we needed to break the cycle of survival mode and learn how to pause and settle so we could engage our children from a place of connection and care rather than reactivity. We define settling as the practice of pausing, slowing things down if necessary, and bringing your awareness into your body and into the present moment where the sacred dwells. As parents, too often we focus only on our children. We can forget to honor our own personal lives as sacred. It is from a cup that overflows that our children will have their thirst quenched.

Psalm 46:10 is a key verse in the Christian contemplative tradition. It instructs us to *be still* because it is only through stillness that we will come to know the truth about God, who lives in us, loves us, and delights in us. Simply put, without stillness, we will too often miss the Divine presence permeating every breath and heartbeat. And that is why so many in the Christian contemplative tradition emphasize the transformational power of becoming truly present to one's life. Brother Lawrence, a contemplative from the seventeenth century, wrote a book entitled *The Practice of the Presence of God*, which he describes as a way of living the miracle of one's own life through "doing little things for the love of God."[3] It seems the contemplatives know something that is true, but all too often neglected—namely, that being fully present cannot be assumed. In fact, many of us are largely absent from the depths of our own experience, because we are too distracted and preoccupied with our inner voices, narratives, and unresolved wounds of our lives. Thankfully, though, presence is a practice that we can cultivate and learn to abide in.

When it comes to parenting, we know that being present can feel like a great challenge. We have bills to pay, mouths to feed, errands to run, houses to clean, and playtimes to supervise. So, how exactly can we begin to approach our entire lives with full presence, rather than a fast attempt to get through each moment and go to the next thing? While the answer is simple, it is not easy. We go moment by moment, and we try again. There are several practices that can be of support to us. The first one, that is receiving a lot of mainstream attention, is that of mindful parenting, created by Jon and Myla Kabat-Zinn.[4] Their approach has been revolutionary for many families because it involves noticing the depths of one's personal experience and how that can open a parent up to noticing the contours of their children's experiences. In short, the more we notice, the more options we have before us to engage compassionately.

According to mindful parenting, the first step is to deliberately slow things down. This is the task of *settling*. In a world that is moving faster by the day, one of the most powerful and revolutionary actions we can take is to pause and settle. For us, settling is a conscious choice to stop reacting or moving from one thing to another and bring more focus to the lived experience of the moment. There are many different ways to settle and slow things down. It does not always look the same. For example, settling can look like intentionally sitting on the sofa to pause and rest or stepping outside to take a few deep breaths. Other times, it looks like lighting a candle or playing soothing music. The intent is to find something that brings comfort and connection amid struggles or stress.

Settling is also a way we create space to call out to God for connection and communion. It is not simply asking for help (although that is part of it). Settling transcends a transactional relationship with the Divine and is simply about being *with* God (who is already with us!) in the mundane moments of our lives. For example, when we make our morning coffee or breakfast, we can choose to be fully aware of that act. We can enjoy a meal together more fully by putting aside our cell phones and consciously eating our food, checking in on how we are feeling and tasting, and allowing our senses to come alive. Of course, many thoughts will attempt to turn our attention away from the moment. If we notice this happening (which is okay and normal!), we simply extend compassion to ourselves and gently return our full attention to what is occurring in front of us.

Another place we practice settling with our family is on the morning drive to school. We invite our kids to share how they are feeling, and we listen with compassion to whatever arises. If time permits, we invite them to offer one hopeful intention or prayer for their day. Our children are not always willing and ready to share, and that is okay too. Our intention is not to impose a spiritual practice onto them, but rather invite them to engage if and when they are ready. The important part is that we remain consistent in our daily invitation to participate and model to them our daily practice of settling into the present moment and into the presence of God.

Settling also offers an invitation to become aware of our breath. In the Bible, the Hebrew word for "spirit" is *ruach*, can also be translated as "breath." Christian contemplatives have offered teachings over many centuries about the connection between our breath and the experience of the Holy. In her book *Breath Prayer*, Christine Valters Paintner shares a variety of breath prayers that can be easily integrated into daily life.[5] A breath prayer combines words or phrases with the rhythm of breathing. Paintner invites us, especially in the challenging moments of our day, to bring awareness to our inhale, to become present to the moment, and with our exhale to breathe out any worry, fear, or anxiety. Through breathing practices like these, we have learned that even a quick moment to become aware of our breath is powerful enough to help us remember how near and accessible God's presence is to us. In a world that is obsessed with motion, give yourself permission to pause, breathe, and settle.

A settling practice: Settle into the presence of your sacred source

The first movement of the SACRED practice is to settle into the presence of your sacred source. This sacred source could be God, the Spirit, the land, a natural element, or an ancestor—whatever source feels supportive to you. If you are newer to the practice of stillness, we invite you to try this practice for just a couple of minutes and, as you feel more comfortable, you can lengthen the time up to five, then ten, fifteen, and even up to thirty minutes.[6] We completely understand as parents how difficult it is to find any time to be still! However, we encourage you to find a moment, even if it's short, when you can take a pause and just be (you deserve it!).

To take this practice one step further, find the same moment each day when you can intentionally practice pausing and settling your awareness into the present moment. For example, in our home, we tend to practice stillness together at night when the kids are already sleeping so there are fewer distractions. However, we understand the spontaneity and surprises that come with parenthood and invite you to be flexible and engage in this practice at literally any point throughout the day that works best for you.

To begin this practice, take an intentional pause and gently bring awareness to your breath. Then, position your body in a posture that feels both relaxed and aware.

Allow yourself to breathe in a way that feels natural and right to you. Let each breath be a reminder that you are infinitely loved.

When thoughts of the past or future enter your mind, gently let each thought go and return to your breath. If you need more support, find a word or phrase you can return to as an anchor whenever you notice a thought arise. For example, you might choose the word "love." Gently say this word whenever you notice your mind wander. When you say your word, return your awareness back to your breath.

Say your grounding word or phrase as often as you need. The point isn't to stop thinking, but to commit to the practice of gently noticing your thoughts and returning back to the present moment.

Next, bring your awareness into your body. Notice where your body feels any tension, energy, or pain, and gently move your body in a way that feels right to you. You might turn your neck from side to side, gently roll your shoulders back, or roll out tension in your ankles. Trust your body to guide your movement.

Invite your sacred source to accompany you. Your sacred source could be God, the Spirit, the land, a natural element, or an ancestor. Identify which sacred source feels supportive to you in this moment. Continue to keep your awareness on your sacred source. You might visualize an image or recite a scripture or mantra that helps you experience the sacred presence. Settle into the sacred presence just as you are with no agenda.

After a few minutes, whenever you feel ready, offer gratitude to your sacred source for accompanying you. Gently bring awareness back to your breath, then to your body, then to the physical space you are in.

End by offering gratitude to yourself for this gift of experiencing sacred stillness. If it feels right, you can place your hands on your heart, take a small bow, or place your hands on your lower abdomen as a sign of gratitude and honor for the sacred encounter.

Remember, this practice has no set time limit. If this is your first time experiencing stillness, you can try this practice for just a couple of minutes and then increase the number of minutes over time as you feel ready and comfortable.

We encourage you to also consider pausing and settling into your breath at any point in the day, even for just three seconds! Whether you are alone, in a quiet place, or surrounded by chaos, you can always practice bringing your awareness to your breath and body and inviting your sacred source to accompany you. The intention is to simply *be* and practice being open to experiencing life as it is (and not how we think it should be).

Intercultural perspective on settling

Settling into our own personhood sounds a lot like accepting our individuality. While settling can include self-acceptance, it's really getting at something deeper. Our personhood is trinitarian—meaning, our deepest identity is relational. In the Christian tradition, the Trinity is a symbol of the radical relatedness of God through the three persons of the Father, the Son, and Holy Spirit. Because God is the Creator, this trinitarian nature is reflected in all of reality. Because we are made in the image of God, we are called to live out this radical relatedness to all of life. Radical relatedness means we can honor our differences rather than erase or hide them.

How do we know that our identities are radically related? Take, for example, the identity of being a parent—it applies only because one has had a child. Ethnicity is another form of identity and is embedded in the people and communities we come from. Another example might be that of being a Christian—the identity is rooted in the person named Jesus of Nazareth whom we look to as a guide and exemplar for our lives. All the parts of our identity are made possible because of the relationships we have with others. When we see our identities as continuously formed by others, we begin to see the trinitarian nature of all life. This has important implications for intercultural relationships. A trinitarian approach to intercultural households leads us to truly listen and learn from others' cultural perspectives rather than staying closed off or judgmental of them.

The more we have studied and learned about the cultural practices of our ancestors, the more we have become open to and even supported by diverse cultural practices that allow us to connect to our sacred source. Some of these practices include dancing to cultural music, gardening and caring for plants, creating sacred altars in our home, and eating together. We have also learned to call on the wisdom of our ancestors for support. This is as simple as inviting them consciously into our awareness through prayer or through rituals such as Día de los Muertos, where we remember their lives and make offerings of welcome and gratitude for the wisdom, care, and spirit they imparted to us. In the transfiguration of Jesus in Matthew 17:1–9, Jesus engages a similar practice as he communes with Moses and Elijah and receives the word from the cloud: "This is my Son, the Beloved; with him I am well pleased; listen to him!" In Hebrews 12, the apostle Paul describes the ancestors who have preceded us as the "cloud of witnesses" who surround us and buoy us in faith.

We are grateful for various models that can support a connection with ancestral wisdom, such as the one created by Paul Smith at the Integral Christian Network (ICN).[7] The ICN teaches that our experiences are profoundly interconnected with all those who have come before us, and it is important to be open to connecting with them. For us, growing in wisdom and compassion has been strengthened by making room in our lives to be supported by those who have come before us both biologically and spiritually. Ancestral connection has always been a predominant spiritual practice by communities of the global majority, a practice that has been historically demonized by colonial versions of European Christianity. In sum, we affirm the manifold cultural wisdom, practices, and traditions with which our people have found a sense of centeredness for many generations.

Helping our children settle

One of the most difficult times to be a parent is in the middle of the night when your child wakes you up from a deep sleep. As many of you know, being a parent of young children is physically demanding, and sleep deprivation is very real. Knowing this, we have learned to create intentional time during the week to rest and restore our energy. We often commit to Sundays being a day of rest (or Sabbath) for the whole family where we do not have to perform or work and can simply enjoy being together. We also are intentional not to overschedule our family calendar so that we have at least two weeknights open where we do not have to be at any event. (With four kids this can be a challenge!)

Even with these efforts, we can still struggle to feel rested, and we have accepted the reality that in this season while our kids are so young, we will experience interrupted sleep. One night while everyone was in bed, the house was quiet. We fell asleep to the soft buzzing of the kids' sound machine in their room down the hall. I (Neddy) tend to be the lightest sleeper, and just a few hours later, in the darkest and stillest moment of the night, I heard the faint cries of our six-year-old. After taking a few deep breaths to wake my body up from sleep, I walked over to our son's bedroom as his cries became louder and louder.

I sat next to him on his bed and said, "I'm here. How can I help you?" But his tiredness and frustration took over and quickly escalated. At a young age like six, intense emotions are real (and developmentally appropriate). Even in our best attempts to stay calm and defuse these situations, a child's emotions still often take over. When we are unable to calm our children with our words and actions alone, what else can we do but settle into the moment?

Through lots of reflection, practice, and mistakes, we have learned the power of entering these situations committed to being a grounding presence for our children. This is much easier said than done. When they are unable to regulate themselves, it's our job as parents to hold the space with safety and compassion as a place of refuge. Is that not what God provides for us?

We have found that when we consistently practice moments of settling into our breath and leaning into our spiritual resources throughout our day, we have more capacity to be a safe and grounding presence for our children in their most difficult moments. This might feel challenging or unattainable for you—it did to us too. However, through the power of consistent spiritual practice, we have developed a greater capacity to respond to our children from a place grounded in love. Our spiritual practice connects us to the infinite love of the Divine and empowers us to offer the same love to our children. Challenging moments like the one we've described can feel especially difficult if your parent or caregiver could not lovingly hold space for you when you were a child. We encourage you to trust that through your spiritual practice, transformation of the heart will take place. It's a journey and not a race.

While our six-year-old son cried louder and louder, I did my best to keep him safe and stay grounded, letting him know that I was there to help. At some point when our children are ready, their emotions slowly begin to pass and their bodies naturally begin to settle. Once they have relaxed, their awareness settles into our presence, and almost every time they lean in for a hug. It's as though their bodies are communicating, *You're still here with me, thank you.* When our children feel ready for an embrace, in these moments, saying a simple "I love you and I'm here with you" goes a long way, because it shows our children that in all circumstances, love is available to them.

Children naturally think in ways that are intuitive. Because their rational minds are still developing, they sense their reality more heavily in their bodies and emotions. Their body language and emotions can give us key information on how we can best show up for them. There was another instance when our four-year-old was throwing toys, knocking over household items, and saying hurtful phrases to us and his siblings. Rather than assuming he was choosing to be defiant, we attempted to notice what he was feeling and offer him support. I (Aizaiah) looked at him and said, "I notice you're throwing toys. It seems like you're feeling frustrated." Even though we were there ready to help, he wasn't ready to receive it.

Children are not always ready to be helped, and part of learning to settle is learning how to be lovingly present to them where *they* are at. That day with our four-year-old, we made several more attempts to validate his frustration. After a couple of hours, he finally sighed and blurted out, "I feel like I can't make my own choices!" In that moment, it became crystal clear why he was throwing toys and saying hurtful phrases. His behavior was communicating an unmet need, the need to feel like he had the power to make a choice. With this newfound realization, I offered him my physical presence, and our four-year-old leaned in for a hug. "It is very important to us that you can make your own choices," I said. "When you feel ready, we would like to support you in doing that."

As parents, the commitment to settle into our sacred source is necessary and powerful for cultivating a sense of safety for our children so they feel empowered to grow, learn, and be their truest selves. When our children feel our groundedness, they are more able to become aware of their experiences and articulate what they are feeling. Again, this takes time; it's a lifelong journey. But when our children do feel safe enough to share what they feel, we celebrate.

The practice of settling is something we invite you to embrace in both the joyous and the difficult moments. We find that, especially in difficult moments, settling into our sacred source empowers us to act and respond from a loving and free state. We realize we don't have to repeat patterns or cycles from pain that has been passed down to us from our own childhood experiences. Rather, our hope is to be inspired and empowered by the Divine; to parent from a liberated place. Furthermore, when we practice settling into the presence of the sacred in the calm and joyous moments, it's as though we are filling up our hearts, increasing our capacity to remain more grounded during the challenging ones. When settling becomes a daily practice, we learn to let go of what is not necessary so that God can be revealed to us anew. Settling then can refresh our ability to hear from God and when we least expect it, love will flow like an everlasting stream.

Other ways to practice settling

This list of ideas is not exhaustive, but we offer them as a starting point for ways to engage settling throughout the day. Feel free to adapt these for your context.

Handwashing or bathing

The task of handwashing or bathing can be an opportune moment to settle in and bring your awareness to your sacred source.[8] In the Christian scriptures, God is often referred to as Living Water. As you wash your hands or body, offer gratitude to God for the gift of water and the gift of life. You can model this gratitude to your children and practice it with them too.

Conscious walk or stroll

Going outside every day, even if only for a short time, has a tremendous impact on our ability to connect to God and ourselves. Being in the natural world can help us be more open and receptive to the spaciousness and groundedness of the Divine's presence. As you take a walk or stroll outside, notice how your senses are activated. Can you feel the wind on your skin, the sun's warmth on your face? What can you smell? Hear? Feel? This is a wonderful grounding practice for parents and children to experience the gift of *being* together.

Zen walking meditation

Practice walking slowly in the same rhythm as your breath. Move with gentleness and ease allowing your whole heart to be given to each step. This practice helps you become present within yourself and in the practice of walking.[9]

Listening or moving to music

As you listen to music that resonates with your soul, notice how songs can bring a sense of safety and refuge. Be intentional about playing this music in your home when you feel tired, disconnected, or empty. Also, play this music with your children and share with them how the lyrics or music make you feel. You can also ask your children what songs help them feel safe and calm and create a family playlist.

Create a sacred space or altar

Invite your children to create a sacred space or altar with you inside or outside of your home. Consider what natural elements, icons, stones, and images will foster a sense of welcome, inspiration, and connection to the Divine. When your child offers an idea, be open to welcoming the unique ways they understand and relate to the Divine. Commit to a weekly or monthly rhythm of devoting time together at the sacred space to reflect together and pray.

Settle into a story

We have created a weekly rhythm where we open a Bible story together and explore the story as a family.[10] As the parents, we hold the space with openness and begin to read the story. Meanwhile our children are invited to share what they notice, act out a scene, or ask questions. Our children are young and oftentimes cannot sit still, and that is okay! There is no agenda for this practice. It is purely a way to experience a story together in the authenticity of your home, at whatever level your children can. We encourage you to listen deeply to what your children share and be open to learning from them!

This practice does not need to be limited to Bible stories. There are many incredible authors who have written inspiring stories for children, and we encourage you to explore stories like these with your family. If this is a new practice for your family, your children may not be as engaged at first (this was the case for us). However, with patience and consistency, your children will begin to recognize when it's time for a story, and they will begin to connect to this practice and find meaning in it.

3

Acknowledge

Or do you not know that your body is a temple of the Holy Spirit within you . . .?
—1 Corinthians 6:19

It was a clear morning when I (Neddy) stopped at a red light on our drive to school. Even with the warmth of the sunshine piercing through the windows, the car ride still felt tense because we were running a little later than usual. Our oldest child, no longer able to hold back her frustration, said, "We're late and it's all my brother's fault!" I could empathize with her frustration, as I really do not like being late either. I said as calmly as I could, "It is a hard feeling to be late, and we are late today because we needed a little bit of extra time to take care of our bodies this morning."

Our six-year-old son then blurted out, "Our bodies are special and important!"

"Yes, they are!" I replied. "And why are our bodies special and important?"

"Because then we couldn't be alive!" he said.

Our eldest took a deep sigh and responded, "I guess it is important to take care of our bodies." Although we were running late, I was glad for a moment where we could learn the importance of taking our time to tend to our bodies each day.

Throughout our parenting journey, we have learned to place greater value on our relationship to our bodies and have had to unlearn many of the dominant interpretations of the Christian scriptures that claim we should suppress our bodily desires because our flesh is sinful in nature.

The supposed split between the body and spirit is age-old in Western culture. Its origins are the philosophy of Plato, who taught that our soul was completely separate from our body. For Plato, the body was destined to die, but the soul was eternal. In the fervor of the scientific revolution between the sixteenth and seventeenth centuries, proponents of rationalism took the idea that a soul was superior to the body and replaced it with the idea that the mind was the highest aspect of a person. All these ideas reached their peak in the words of mathematician and philosopher Rene Descartes, who declared "Cogito, ergo sum"—I think, therefore I am. This perceived split between mind and body has only accelerated, leading us to live more and more fragmented lives.

Today, many in the West follow Cartesian thinking, believing that what is "good" are only those aspects of our intellect that are individualized, autonomous, rational, and self-reliant. We have been seduced by the power of our intellect, and that is why we are stunned by things like supercomputers, algorithms, supersonic speed, and artificial intelligence. We believe faster and bigger is always better. We believe our created technologies will "save us" and take away our pain. Yet in some ways, technologies have weakened our capacity to transform suffering. This transformation is something that our ancestors have cultivated over many millennia. My (Neddy's) grandmother, for example, was a young migrant farmworker in the

United States who spoke little to no English. Her body was pushed to the limit as she carried five babies and continued to work as much as she could so that her family could survive. My grandmother shared that while working in the fields and feeling the soreness and pain of her body, she would look to the sun and begin to sing a song of praise, trusting that God would give her the strength she needed for the day. Her practice of facing the sun and opening her heart to sing allowed her body to experience a deep transformation. Her suffering was transformed into her innate capacity to connect to nature and God.

Today, instead of trusting in our embodied wisdom, we look to the internet for more information. We have forgotten that all technologies are simply tools and must be used with discernment, rather than as a means of escaping from our lives. While it may sound like we are rejecting technology, we actually believe that technology can bring a lot of good. We simply want people to become aware of *how* we relate to technology so that we can realize freedom comes from skillfully using technology rather than unconsciously allowing technology to use us. Although the supremacy of the intellect began in the Western Hemisphere, it is quickly spreading to every corner of the globe thanks to globalization. And, in modern times, we have collectively inherited cultures that demonize all other forms of embodied knowledge, such as insight that comes from our emotions, bodily sensations, intuitions, cosmic connection, ancestral knowledge, or spiritual insights.

For people of the global majority, our bodies, languages, and cultural forms of wisdom are often viewed as inferior and untrustworthy. We believe these must be reclaimed if we are to live in wholeness. Bishop Yvette Flunder talks about healing from "oppression sickness" that has been passed down because of colonial Christianity. She describes oppression sickness as "internalized oppression that causes the oppressed to be infected by the sickness of the oppressor."[1] When oppression is internalized, it further oppresses minoritized people. "Oppression sickness" is the result of teachings that have used the Bible to enslave, condemn, and internalize a self-hatred of our lived experiences. You may be familiar with this yourself. Many strands of Christianity emphasize "right belief" as though there were only one correct cultural interpretation of Christianity. As a result of these teachings, many of us have been taught that God detests our bodies because they are inherently sinful and carry unrelenting passions that distract us from God.

Reconnecting with our bodies

Thankfully, we can remember that God is present and glorified by attending to our lives (and bodies). In the second century, Irenaeus, bishop of Lyons, proclaimed, "The glory of God is the living human and the life of the human is the vision of God."[2] For Irenaeus, God's glory is powerfully revealed when a human embraces the fullness of their experience, which is made possible through the Divine's help. In chapter 1, we named the underlying assumption of belovedness: that life is inherently precious to God. From the story of creation in Genesis 1, we know that the body is beautiful and sacred, worthy of attention and affection. The apostle Paul echoes this sentiment with his very high view of the body, telling the Corinthian church that the body is the "temple," or dwelling place, of the Holy Spirit. This powerful assertion from Paul can help teach us to listen and tend to our bodies so that we can be in greater alignment with the Spirit. Additionally, when we listen to our bodies, we begin to learn what our needs are and how we can join God in extending compassion to them so that the glory of God may be revealed.

To remember our bodies are the dwelling place of the Spirit, we need to unlearn (and heal) all that has been passed down unnoticed to the next generation.[3] Epigenetics research demonstrates that our bodies inherit the stressors of previous generations. These inheritances are reinforced through our autonomic nervous system (ANS). *Autonomic* refers to automatic, meaning that the ANS automatically regulates bodily processes (like heart rate, blood pressure, breathing, and digestion). However, our ANS processes are deeply impacted by those we are in close relationship with. If our ANS is too overwhelmed, we will often end up acting in ways that are harmful to ourselves or others. According to child psychologist Daniel Siegel, each of us has a "window of tolerance" where we can grow and be in healthy relationships with others.[4] If the window is not honored, then we will move into psychological states that are closed off to others, and cycles of inherited stress will prevail.

There are three primary things to understand about the autonomic nervous system. First, it is malleable and can quickly change in response to those around us. For example, if we are near someone who is experiencing a calm, openhearted state, they can help us regain our own sense of calm. On the other hand, if those around us are anxious, it can easily make us feel more anxious. The bottom line is that our ANS is constantly scanning our environments for threats. It can be either triggered or not depending on the states of others who are around us.

Second, the ANS works below the level of consciousness. Our ANS responses take place without our even thinking about it. This is actually a gift—in some cases, that unconscious response could be the difference between life and death. The problem, however, is that sometimes our ANS incorrectly perceives a life-and-death threat. For example, if our kids have a meltdown when we are already feeling exhausted, our ANS is likely to respond more harshly or apathetically. It's primed to keep us alive and respond to threats, but a meltdown is not actually a life-and-death situation. It may just be that we need space for rest.

Third, to return to its window of tolerance, our ANS needs different things depending on each situation. While each of us reacts differently in diverse situations, in some cases, our ANS will thrust us into overdrive, or what neuroscientists call "hyperarousal." When we are in a state of hyperarousal, we do all that we can to fight back or act decisively to return to our window of tolerance. In other cases, however, our ANS downregulates our body and tells us to do less with the stress we are perceiving. Neuroscientists call this "hypoarousal," or a "freeze" state.

As we know, being over or under reactive may have certain survival benefits, but it may not lead us to the most desirable actions as parents. And ultimately, our spiritual work is to become aware of our ANS processes, and even to find ways of calming our ANS personally and relationally. Only when our ANS is tended to compassionately can we discern what response is most life-giving and will yield true and lasting transformation and healing. In order to do this, we must learn to engage ourselves from a state of openhearted clarity and compassion. The good news is that our ANS can be strengthened through spiritual practices that build our resilience to deal with stressors as they arise. A few examples of this include paying attention to when more vulnerable parts within us are triggered, or activated, and being curious about them rather than judgmental. Our ANS can also be strengthened physiologically by staying well-hydrated and rested.

Although the habit of disregarding our body is ingrained by dominant culture, it can be unlearned. New ways of being and relating to one another *are* possible. If we are to parent from a place of connection and transformation, then we must become aware of when our bodies are communicating a need, rather than taking the easy route of ignoring or suppressing it. It takes great intention to honor our bodies in our chaotic world. Dominant culture wants us to focus on results and productivity, and we so easily deny the very temple, our body, which allows us to feel love and experience life.

Modern contemplative Cynthia Bourgeault depicts Mary Magdalene as a disciple of Jesus who knew him to be fully embodied and "earthy."[5] In the Christian West, Mary Magdalene is often overlooked even though she is one of the most advanced and intimate disciples of Jesus, perhaps because she is usually portrayed as a repentant prostitute from whom Jesus cast out seven demons.[6] For Bourgeault, however, Mary's relationship with Jesus shows that God does not lead us toward shame or denial of the body or its needs. Instead, Jesus practiced and taught a way for each of us to embrace our whole selves, including our bodies, in love. We need a sacred view of the body if we are to grow into our practice of *acknowledging*, but this perspective also expands our view of the many ways our bodies communicate. Whether through sensations, intuitions, or feelings, each embodied message has a place.

All of this greatly influences our parenting, for anything we do not learn to acknowledge in ourselves will be projected onto our children (or our partners). Projection happens when we identify *others* as the source of the problem rather than turning within first to identify what is going on inside of us.

If we do not take time to tend to our inner experiences, we will easily get caught in a hero-victim cycle. This cycle fixes us into perceived roles of either being the hero or being the victim of others' choices. Neither, however, is ultimately true. Believing we are totally one or the other has devastating consequences on our spiritual life and mental health. In fact, the hero-victim cycle is at its worst when we "succeed" at being a "hero" parent, because we start to believe that the worth of our parenthood is only connected to results or outcomes rather than the mercy of God, which invites us on an ongoing journey of discovering love more deeply even through our shortcomings.

In our spiritual life, we know that failure, not success, is often where we learn the most and where we discover grace. Christian contemplative Richard Rohr calls the process of learning to meet God in our mess-ups "falling upward." "God knows that all of us will fall somehow," he writes, "God must say after each failure of ours, 'Oh, here is a great opportunity! Let's see how we can work with this!' After our ego-inflating successes, God surely says, 'Well, nothing new or good is going to happen here!' Failure and suffering are the great equalizers and levelers among humans."[7] According to Rohr, God is not out to punish us for our mistakes. God wants to teach us more deeply about how profoundly we are loved and cared for. Each detail of our experience is important to God, and God loves to provide for our needs (Psalm 139:14; Matthew 7:11).

We hope it is clear we are not promoting the idea that we should seek failure (life will naturally bring failure to us along the way!). Rather, we seek to open ourselves continually to God, whose power is made perfect in our weakness (2 Corinthians 12:9). As parents, then, our desire is to demonstrate to our children that we are not out to punish them when they fail. We are committed to showing up in love when they experience hardship or pain in their mess-ups and vulnerabilities.

An acknowledging practice: Notice and acknowledge thoughts, emotions, and bodily sensations

This acknowledgment practice helps develop a greater inner capacity to be present to life through the lens of love. Because true love does not seek to impose an agenda, but rather is present to life as it naturally flows. When we practice noticing our real experience and can bear loving witness to it, we connect to the greater Source of Love in us that cares for us in all circumstances.

This practice can be adapted to support you wherever you are. It can take a few minutes or up to thirty minutes. You are invited to engage it the way it best supports you.

> To begin, you are invited to find your inner grounding by connecting to your sacred source, as described in the previous chapter on settling.
>
> Then, in a posture of stillness and receptivity, simply begin to notice what thoughts, emotions, or bodily sensations you are experiencing. Do not rush yourself. Simply notice what you are experiencing.
>
> If you notice your mind getting distracted by thoughts of the past or future, simply bring awareness back to your breath, allowing your breath to be an anchor for you in the present moment. Gently let go of any inclination to judge yourself during this practice Simply return to your breath, and keep taking note.
>
> As you notice what is coming up for you, is there a thought (or thought pattern) that comes to mind? Take

notice of your thoughts and acknowledge them. If it feels right, you can say to the thought or thought pattern, "I see you, and I'm here."

Is there an emotion or multiple emotions that are surfacing? You can say to each emotion, "I see you, and I'm here."

What is your body experiencing? Any tension, pain, tightness, heat, coolness, tingling, or numbness? You can send loving compassion to the part of your body that is activated and move your body in any way that feels supportive. It might look like swaying side to side, placing your hands over your heart, gently rolling out your neck and shoulders, or stretching, for example.

To each part of you that is showing up, each thought, emotion, or bodily sensation, offer it loving acknowledgment by letting it know that you are here to bear loving witness to its experience. Again, you might say, "I see you, and I'm here."

When you feel ready, gently bring your awareness back to your breath, then your body, and then into the physical space you are in.

Take a final deep breath and offer gratitude to yourself and the Divine for the gift of this experience.

Radical reconstruction

Many of us have been told that God is a separate being in the sky who will severely punish us if we commit an error. If this is true, why would we want to love our bodies? If we believe this, we feel unsafe, surveilled by a harsh judge, and think that we should do our best to cover things up and hide the truth of our experiences. This sounds remarkably like the experience of Adam and Eve early in the book of Genesis. After they had sinned by eating forbidden fruit from the tree of knowledge of good and evil, they attempted to hide themselves from the presence of God. Bound in shame, they felt their choices made them unlovable to God. They believed God to be someone that God was not. But Adam and Eve's understanding of the Divine were upended when God did not punish them for hiding but instead made clothing for them to care for their bodies. As Cole Arthur Riley puts it eloquently, "On the day that the world began to die, God became a seamstress."[8]

God is about restoration and renewal rather than punishment. While Adam and Eve still needed to suffer the consequences of their choices, the story reveals how God did not seek to end their lives but instead sent them to till the ground and learn anew how to walk with God.

God is not a punisher who will treat us well only when we are perfect. Even in our mistakes, God still is bountiful in mercy. The question for each of us—especially as parents—is, do we treat ourselves with the same mercy? Or do we allow self-condemnation to govern our lives? Depending on our response, we can see how the latter would put us in a constantly anxious state hoping that we never slip up. If we are not careful, we can imagine how these self-defeating beliefs can easily trickle into our parenting practices. For example, how often do our children hear us correcting their behavior rather than complimenting them? Or what is our automatic emotional response when our child makes a mistake? Is our response one of compassion or disappointment? When we remember that we are not the sum of all our actions, that we are worth so much more, we increase our capacity as parents to respond to every situation with love. The love in our lives is not defined by our worst moments or even the best ones. Our lovability is a free gift from God. If we can transform our belief in a God who punishes us to that of a God who radically loves us, then we can transform the hierarchical ways of parenting handed to us by dominant culture to one of mutuality, dignity, and respect. If we know that God loves us, then how much more does God love our children? Our parenthood is deeply transformed when our beliefs about the Divine are centered on divine mercy rather than judgment. "Mercy triumphs over judgment," says James 2:13.

Our own beliefs about the Divine have had to be radically reconstructed. We are grateful to the Christian contemplatives we have read and had the privilege to meet who have modeled alternatives. They have asked us three primary questions when it comes to reorienting our relationship to God: What do we ultimately want? Who is the Divine? And how does the Divine see us?

One of the most influential examples is the great spiritual leader of the civil rights movement in the United States, Howard Thurman. Thurman describes the experience of belovedness at the core of Jesus' teaching. For Thurman, an African American living in the terror of racial oppression in the United States, it was critical for him to know his own life (which the dominant society oppressed) as beloved. Thurman did not see God as the punisher of life but the Love who embraces life. Thurman points out that one of Jesus' most transformational moments with the Divine appears during his baptism when he is told, "This is my Son, the beloved, with whom I am well pleased" (Matthew 3:17). This profound experience of divine parental acceptance and care grounded Jesus, a grounding that he continually returned to in prayer (Luke 6:12; Matthew

14:23; Mark 6:46). Furthermore, Jesus performed his entire ministry from his own experiential knowledge of belovedness, and this wisdom guided all his interactions with others (including human and the more-than-human life), especially those whom society rejected. Simply put, Jesus saw belovedness in every being and in all that he saw. And he invited others to live in this experience that was radically different from the oppressive cycles of empire.

If we follow Thurman and believe Christianity is truly a religion of holistic liberation, then we must become aware of the aspects of our lives that we were taught were evil, whether they be our cultural heritage, our fears, or even our worries. We can also consider our bodies. Particularly in the United States, legacies of colonial oppression have ingrained in communities of color a negative view of their own bodies. We will find, however, that no two bodies are similar and that each of us is indeed "fearfully and wonderfully made" (Psalm 139:14). When we embrace the diverse aspects of our embodied experiences, it impacts how we relate to diversity around us. In an increasingly diverse world, we *must* learn how to honor and welcome diverse peoples and views. And that begins with listening to the diversity of our own bodily knowledge. When we acknowledge and welcome our whole selves, including our bodies, we begin to see how our parenting transforms into a practice of sharing divine love, rather than a role to perform in perfection.

For all of us who come from marginalized backgrounds (in our case, immigrant families who were migrant farmworkers seeking to provide for their families), this is a huge turn toward perceiving that our own experiences contain wisdom in their own right. We do not have to look to the "experts" or other more accomplished people to find the dwelling place of the Holy. It begins right inside and among each of us. In our families, we are so grateful for how our grandparents modeled a hard work ethic. But this was often at the expense of their bodily needs. Because they lived in poverty, they did not receive the same access to care as others, nor did they have the support or space to truly listen to their bodies' needs. Their bodies were treated like machines, by those with more material resources, to build wealth for others, rather than as a way to freely and personally experience their humanity. In our healing path, we have begun to consciously choose to honor our bodies as beloved and trust in the radical love and mercy of God. What we've discovered is that this path offers us greater support as parents to show up more fully and compassionately to our children.

The welcoming prayer

When we practice acknowledging, we begin to understand that, while our lives are imperfect, they are filled with experiences that have wisdom to offer. The movement of acknowledgment in the SACRED practice is the invitation to simply notice cycles and patterns within ourselves so that we can compassionately learn from them and not be so easily led by them. The key in all of this is to not judge ourselves but to simply notice and let go. Letting go is different from ignoring or rejecting something or making war. Letting go is a practice of entrusting our full lives to God—including the things we would rather not be true. When we do this, we begin to see not only that love was with us all along, but that it enlarges our capacity for ever-expanding compassion toward the world.

A powerful contemplative practice that helps us acknowledge our lived experience is the "Welcoming Prayer" made popular by Father Thomas Keating. This prayer is also known as centering prayer. It is essentially a way of praying that involves noticing whatever thought, feeling, or sensation arises in our experience without getting attached or stuck to it. Once we can acknowledge what is present, we are invited to let it go, recognizing that our communion with the Divine is less about what we do or do not do and instead is received as a free gift. Our living spirituality is one of relational dynamism rather than fixed ideas or petty preoccupations.

When we first started practicing centering prayer, it felt miserable. We had countless thoughts, feelings, and sensations, and when we struggled to stick with it one of our teachers at the time simply replied, "You are lucky to have so many invitations to learn to let go!" It sure did not feel like luck. But with more practice, we learned we were much more than our thoughts. We learned to acknowledge things for what they are rather than what we wanted them to be. As humans, we experience highs and lows, and our emotions can feel like waves in an ocean. But we can learn to notice how our experiences come and go, and what always remains is groundness in love. In our home, for example, life often feels full (imagine four young kids running and screaming!). When something breaks or gets damaged in the house, it's easy to become overwhelmed. The practice of centering prayer helps us notice what we are experiencing and compassionately let go of the urge to scold our child or set unrealistic expectations on them. We can return to a deep love and compassion that grounds us in all circumstances.

Centering prayer encourages us to recognize that everything we encounter is another invitation to deepen our trust in God. When we practice centering prayer, we come to see we have more opportunities to relate to our inner experience (rather than only giving in to what arises or rejecting it). And further, this practice helps us realize that any one aspect of our experience does not carry the final authority over our lives. It is important to note here that there is a big difference between accepting everything and *participating* in the transformation of everything through divine guidance. In the former, we become passive and disengaged. In the latter, we are discerning, open, and humbled before God. We can trust that whatever comes, God offers support and assistance.

In parenting, we experience a certain freedom when we learn to journey through the process, learning that life is more than just the highs and lows. As parents, we must practice showing our children how to acknowledge life as it is and not get stuck with whatever comes our way (because it will all soon pass). Instead, we can learn to flow creatively with the natural current of life. We model this by inviting our children to notice the places they tend to get stuck and showing them how to gently entrust those to God. Once, when our daughter shared her disappointment with a test score, we invited her to notice what she was feeling, validated her experience, and then helped her return to her breath and reminded her that in the hard times, she is still deeply loved. We can trust in God's mercy and grace to provide us with all the support we need. Sometimes this trust comes from within us, sometimes through a friend or another being in life, but regardless of where it comes from, we know that we are not alone. As we practice trusting and letting go, little by little, and often when we least expect it, wisdom arises from within us that is aligned with where God is leading us.

Acknowledgment takes effort but it can often feel effortless because our trust is not in our performance but in the One who loves us and always will. Of course, this does not mean everything is relative or that we are merely passive—on the contrary, the practice of acknowledgment allows us to act in a more wholesome way that does not come from our ego or prideful arrogance. Acknowledgment is about a willingness to invite whatever feels different or unknown, thus it is a practice of radical inclusion. Radical inclusion welcomes all that is, using the power of compassion. When we practice radical inclusion, we do not lead with our assumptions but rather with receptivity to move toward wholeness and healing. Radical inclusion invites us to name what is real and remain open to what love may be calling us to.

We have found this practice also has implications for social healing in the world. Unnecessary pain and violence often result from human fear of what is different or unknown. A posture of radical inclusion at home increases our heart's capacity to remain open with love for all others. So often the change we try to create comes from a place that is ego-driven and looking for answers or solutions based on our agendas and on our terms alone. The practice of acknowledgment, in a spirit of radical inclusion, can free us from the belief that the world is all on our shoulders while still calling us to act where and when we can, as we are led by the Divine.

Helping our children acknowledge

When our children experience a change or transition in the rhythms of home life, the change can feel daunting. For adults, the change may seem small. But, for children, adjustment does not usually come easy.

When our youngest child was about eight months old, we experienced a significant change—instead of one parent working outside the home, now both of us were working. Just a couple of months prior, our older two children started a new school year while the younger two stayed home. To support this new family rhythm, we hired a nanny to take care of the younger two children during the day. About a month into this new rhythm, our three-year-old began to be uneasy whenever our nanny arrived. Although he genuinely loved playing with her, his tiny body stiffened up whenever she knocked on the door. This anxious pattern continued as time went on. One day, when our nanny arrived, I (Neddy) answered the door and greeted her. Our son's body stiffened, he looked over at me and said, "I hate you."

As you can imagine, hearing these words from your child can bring deep discomfort and pain. Especially if you were scolded or punished as a child for saying these words to your caregiver or parent, it can be easy to act out of tiredness or urgency in these moments—to argue with your child or to dismiss him, saying, "You don't mean that" in an effort to end the discomfort. Or it can be easy to say, "I do not have time for this—I need to get to work!" Thankfully though, through a lot of practice and mistakes, we have developed a greater capacity to acknowledge our children in their moments of struggle.

I knelt down at our son's eye level and took a breath. I held the silence for a moment inviting compassion and curiosity to guide me. I felt led to say, "Does it feel hard when mom and dad have to go to work?" He didn't respond right away, but I continued to hold the silence with compassion and stayed with him at his eye level. Then something shifted in his demeanor. His stiffened body relaxed, and he nodded. Then, he took a deep sigh and leaned in for a hug. I held the embrace, responding to what he needed in that moment—a hug. "Thank you for being honest with me," I said. "I'm glad you can share with me how you feel." Our son softly smiled, then slowly turned his attention toward our nanny, ready to begin the next part of his day.

Although the connection felt profound in that moment, we knew that at his young age, adjusting to this new routine would still take some time. But this experience helped us learn the power of responding to our children with empathy and compassion when hurtful words are expressed. We've come to learn that words like "I hate you" are one way a child communicates that what they are experiencing is uncomfortable or difficult for them. We have learned to not take these words personally. Rather, when we hear words like this, we understand this is our children's way of communicating that they are experiencing something difficult, usually an unmet need. One of our primary roles as parents is to help our children learn how to notice their behavior and to notice what they are feeling. When they feel safe and grounded in our presence, then we can work together to discover how we can best support them. And when they are in a calm and connected state, then they are more open to learning and willing to practice more respectful ways of communicating in the future. The power here is in consistency, because our children do not learn new skills overnight. When we continue to model how to notice what they feel and respectfully respond, their ability to communicate grows over time. Our role is to consistently show up with care, continue to offer compassion, and trust that our practice empowers our children to be formed over time into more compassionate and courageous people. Thus, the practice of acknowledgment truly becomes a way of life and not a random act.

It is revolutionary to diligently notice how our children's bodies are communicating. Rather than ignoring or suppressing their bodily experience—which is typical of the dominant culture—we can meet our child in the depth of their experience and invite them to this awareness too. One early, foggy morning we were ready to drop off our kids at school when our first grader suddenly said he didn't want to go. As the other two siblings cheerfully walked into the school gate, our first grader stayed, put his seatbelt on, and said that school was hard and he felt scared. We did our best to show him that we could hear what he was saying to us, and we acknowledged what he was feeling. "We hear you and we will make a plan together to help support you," we said. "Today is a school day, and you must go to school to learn and grow, and we can walk with you to the gate." Our words didn't seem to calm him down at all. Instead, tears began to slowly roll down his cheek. And then he began to snap his fingers—not a common habit! Noticing his fingers snap, I (Aizaiah) said, "Your body wants you to snap your fingers. That's a good way to help. We will snap with you." Together, snapping our fingers, we slowly walked to the school gate.

In this situation, noticing our child's bodily response to fear helped us support him. More importantly, acknowledging out loud what his body was communicating helped him experience the value of being in tune with his body. Oftentimes, when we feel worry or fear, our body is looking for a way to release that tension and let energy flow out of us. We learned years ago from a spiritual director that shaking out our limbs can literally help reset the nervous system.[9] Our hope in sharing this is that parents continue to practice listening to their bodies and the bodies of their children so that we can offer holistic care, love, and compassion in our children's times of need.

Other ways to practice acknowledgment

Wake-up stretch

Whether you're a morning person or a night owl, practice waking up slowly, bringing your awareness to your body.

Notice how your body wants to naturally move and stretch as you wake up. Oftentimes, when we are waking up, our body naturally moves to stretch but we are not always aware of it. Cultivating a practice of bodily awareness as you wake up can help you feel more grounded and connected to yourself as you begin your day. To deepen this practice, greet your body in a spirit of welcome and say aloud, "Good morning, body."

Write it out

Writing a journal entry can be a very effective practice to help you process your inner experience. For some, writing with pen and paper works well, for others typing a note on a phone or computer device works better. The practice of writing out your inner reflections, even if it's short, can help you acknowledge your inner experience with more clarity and feel more connected to God and to yourself.

To deepen this practice, commit to journaling for seven consecutive days, and choose whether the morning, midday, or evening works best for you. If it is helpful, you can also consider writing in response to these prompts: *When did you feel energy today? When did you experience difficulty? What is your invitation for tomorrow?*

Remember, when you write, there is no agenda. This practice is an invitation to simply be present to yourself in love.

Sing it out

In the African American and Mexican American Pentecostal churches we have worshipped at, spontaneous singing is greatly emphasized as a form of worship and prayer to God. This practice can help you not get stuck in your rational mind but rather flow freely as you reflect inward. If it feels right to you, sing out a spontaneous song that feels like a natural outpouring of whatever you are holding in your heart and body. Do not worry about singing song lyrics that make sense, rather allow your reflection to be sung out in a natural free flowing tone and rhythm.

Spontaneous singing can be a fun and creative practice with your children too. You can create a drum-like beat or play an instrumental song and invite your child to sing spontaneously. Whatever comes up in the song is the prayer.

Create a collage

Create a collage with images from recycled magazines or any other crafting supplies you might have. As you browse through images and items, allow yourself to choose whatever is drawing your attention. You do not need a rational explanation for why you chose something. When you are drawn to an image or item, simply cut it out and paste it onto your paper or canvas. Continue this process until you feel your collage is complete. When you have finished, gaze at your collage and notice if any themes, thoughts, or patterns arise that help you make sense of your experience. This is a great practice to engage with your children!

Light a candle

The practice of lighting a candle is familiar to the contemplative Christian tradition. Benedictine monk David Steindl-Rast even says that the act itself is one of prayer.[10] Lighting a candle to acknowledge something special or sacred has been very meaningful for our family.

For this practice, you can light one or multiple candles as an individual or as a family. While you do so, acknowledge an experience, an emotion, or a part of you that is activated. The candlelight can represent God's presence with you as you acknowledge and reflect on your experience. You can then offer a prayer asking God to reveal what your invitation is for today and tomorrow. When your prayer is finished, blow out the candle as a sign that your prayer has been received by God. In our home, our children enjoy (supervised) candle-lighting practices. We encourage you to be open and creative as you discover how candlelight rituals can support your family.

Acknowledging dreams

In the Christian tradition as well as other spiritual traditions, the Divine is revealed through dreams. When you wake up from a dream, take a moment to acknowledge the dream and notice what feelings, information, or insights come to you. If it feels right, offer God a prayer with an open heart to receive what God might be revealing to you through your dream.

Invite your children to share their dreams with you, too, and offer them a deep listening presence as they share. Help them discover what emotions or thoughts the dream invoked for them. Remember to be open to hearing anything (as dreams are filled with spontaneity) and teach your children to pray asking God/the Divine for insight into what the dream might be revealing to them.

Meditation on the autonomic nervous system (ANS)

As you begin, consider a time when you felt overly activated and a desire to act or change the situation. To avoid overwhelming your system, focus on a situation that is only mildly uncomfortable. Take a moment to check in with your body and notice how your body felt during that moment. Next, become aware of how this moment affected your eating habits. Did you eat more or less? Then, inquire how this state impacted your sleep. Lastly, consider how this state influenced your use of substances of any kind. In the last step, ask yourself what you believed about God and the world when you were in this state.

In the next phase, repeat the same process, but this time consider a time when you felt disempowered to act or engage. You want to find a time when you felt little energy to do anything at all. Again, focus on a situation that is only mildly triggering so as not to overwhelm your system. Take a moment to check in with your body and notice how your body felt during that moment. Next, become aware of how this moment affected your eating habits. Did you eat more or less? Then, inquire how this state impacted your sleep. Lastly, consider how this state influenced your use of substances of any kind. In the last step, ask yourself what you believed about God and the world when you were in this state.

For the final phase, repeat the process—but now consider a time when you felt grounded, centered, and calm. Take a moment to check in with your body. Notice how your body felt during that moment. Next, become aware of how this moment affected your eating habits. Did you eat more or less? Then, inquire how this state impacted your sleep. Lastly, consider how this state influenced your use of substances of any kind. In the last step, ask yourself what you believe about God and the world when you were in this state.

Notice and reflect on how your body, mind, and spirit changed in these three different states.

4

Curiosity

It is the glory of God to conceal things, but the glory of kings is to search things out.

—Proverbs 25:2

All our children were born in areas of California where snow was just a fantasy. We traveled to Washington state for the holidays, and when our four-year-old daughter touched snow for the first time, her eyes widened with excitement. She began to explore the snow by stomping on it, rolling it in her hands, and even attempting to eat it. Then she asked, "Can we take the snow with us to California?" Her curiosity and amazement were truly fun to watch, and when we shared with her that snow couldn't travel with us to a warmer climate, she was determined to try by placing large chunks of snow in her little pockets.

Our children continually teach us about curiosity. Whether they are attempting to jump off our couches imagining they can fly or venturing without their parents in the middle of a crowded mall, our children naturally investigate their surroundings and are constantly inquisitive about life and their role in it. Psychotherapist and rabbi Steven Rosman writes,

"Children's spirituality is evidenced by their curiosity, their penchant for asking all kinds of questions about where something comes from or why it is the way it is, and their innocent appreciation of the world around them, which some might call worshipful."[1] This powerfully reminds us how our children have so much to teach us about the gift of curiosity. Their natural discovery of reality is also reflective of the greatness of God. As the wisdom of King Solomon attests in Proverbs 25:2, it is the glory of our lives to be curious and discover the many layers of God's wonder through our lived experiences.

It is so easy in the age of algorithms to become mindless and distracted. If we are not careful, we allow predetermined and targeted marketing campaigns to influence us toward behaviors that increase wealth for some people but leave most of us hollow within. We have learned a powerful antidote to this from our children: returning to curiosity. We imagine curiosity as a stance of the heart which is sincere. The word *sincere* derives from words meaning "clean" or "pure." In other words, a heart that is sincere is one that is able to be surprised, bewildered, and astonished by life. Curiosity is the bridge that leads us to awe, which is one of the primary factors associated with transformation and growth.[2] When we live with amazement before life, we can improve our mental health, performance, and creativity.[3] Our curiosity for life can lead us to discover growth, beauty, and connection in ways we never imagined.

Curiosity and transformation

The Internal Family Systems model is a therapeutic tool that describes every person as a system of inner parts led by a core "Self." The Self is the inner resource available to all of us that promotes wholeness inside ourselves.[4] In IFS, the mind is multiple. This does not mean we have multiple personalities, but rather that each of us has a diverse set of interior movements that accompany us throughout the day. If you have ever seen the *Inside Out* films, it is quite similar to that! In IFS, these interior movements are known as "parts" that form our "internal family," and they each carry wisdom and insight for us. Some parts bear woundedness from past experiences; others may be protective toward the Self—or both. When we are willing to listen to the stories of the parts within, we are more able to understand the roots of our experiences. As a therapeutic model (which we have applied through many sessions of personal therapy), IFS creates a connection between the inner self and the outer world by helping people access their Self and come to understand and ultimately heal their varied internal parts.

IFS identifies eight qualities that describe the power of the Self: compassion, creativity, curiosity, confidence, courage, calm, connectedness, and clarity. Curiosity always stands out to us the most because it is unassuming, openhearted, and nonjudgmental. In IFS therapy, the work of healing is only possible when genuine curiosity bubbles up from the person seeking psychological support and the psychologist. Without curiosity, there is only defensiveness, close-mindedness, and a never-ending loop of suffering.

Curiosity helps us discover the roots of our problems rather than just focusing on the symptoms. It helps us connect with each aspect of ourselves in compassion rather than self-hatred or self-loathing. Self-loathing can be especially destructive in the lives of those who are marginalized because we often find ourselves living in a world that wants to make us change who we are to fit in or be accepted. This stems from the deep history of how colonial forces, mixed with the Christian religion, spread throughout the Western world and sought to instill control of others, teaching the false dogma that faith never doubts. Colonial Christianity makes no room for mistakes or questions because it espouses that God has already predetermined who is valuable and who is not and who should be in charge (due to their possession of the truth) and who should be converted. We are not taught to love ourselves, our language, our culture, or our bodies as they are. Curiosity can help us learn why we have sacrificed so much. Hint—it is often for survival!

Through curiosity, we can find both the strength to compassionately accept what has happened and the courage to reclaim and remember those aspects of our lives that we can otherwise be tempted to discard or reject. However, in learning to be completely honest with God, with our wrestlings and doubts, we've seen how our curiosity actually reflects a greater trust in God rather than a lack of trust. We trust that God is loving enough and compassionate enough to care for us in all circumstances. We trust that God's love toward us does not depend on our having all the answers. The power of God's love is that we are deeply cared for even in our confusion and worry. Haven't we seen in our own lives that love is most powerfully expressed when we have the courage to be more vulnerable with one another and that vulnerability is met with compassion rather than contempt? It is amazing how our perspectives can change when we get curious. Curiosity is powerful, and each time we have witnessed it, we find that we learn completely new things about ourselves, others, and even God.

Curiosity requires full humility because it assumes we do not know everything. It assumes there is something life-affirming to discover. In our spiritual journeys, one of the most liberating moments is when we can learn to approach the mystery of God with curiosity rather than certainty. If we can do this, we will find God's comfort being granted to us amid the unknown.

Although we have only been parents for a decade, each step of the journey has felt like another step toward the beyond. Thankfully, cultivating a living relationship with a living God means that we are always ready to find out something new and to be surprised. We have felt so much more free to live out a humble faith where our questions and curiosities are welcome before God. Writer Anne Lamott boldly declares that "the opposite of faith is not doubt, but certainty."[5] Perhaps Lamott is right. Certainty is no faith at all.

A curiosity practice: Listen to the stories of the parts within

This movement of the SACRED practice is partly inspired by the IFS model which asserts there are multiple ego-states, or "parts" within each person. The problem according to IFS is that our parts are polarized. Yet, when we are willing to listen to the stories of the parts within ourselves, we are more able to understand our own experiences. We can then draw on the insight of our internal parts and their needs. Our compassionate curiosity helps us discover the wisdom within, and we learn to trust in what we receive.

The practice we are inviting you to is not a replacement for IFS therapy, which we recommend, but is simply an introduction to connecting with your internal parts. If this practice feels completely new and challenging, that is absolutely okay. With more practice, it becomes easier to connect to your inner parts. Taking the first step in being willing to identify your internal parts goes a long way to start. No matter where you are in your journey, you can always offer yourself compassion and honor.

In this movement of the practice, begin by inviting your sacred source to accompany you. Once you are in a grounded state, one that is calm, compassionate, and curious, notice what part of you (a thought, emotion, or bodily sensation) seems to carry the most energy and is drawing your attention the most. Note that if you do not feel curiosity, see if you can get curious first rather than pressing on.

When you have acknowledged a part of you that you want to explore more deeply and you are feeling curious about it, let this part of yourself know that you are willing to get to know it. You might ask this part of yourself, "If you could talk, what would you want to share? I'm here to listen."

Remain in a posture of stillness and receptivity, deeply listen to what this part of you is communicating. Does it have a story? Is there a memory associated with it? Where did it originate from? What beliefs or assumptions does it carry?

You can dialogue internally with this part, or if it helps, you can write out what information you are gathering from it.

When you feel that this part of you has finished sharing its story, ask it, "What are you longing for? And how can I support you?"

Remain openhearted and willing to listen to how this part of you is seeking your support and care. It might be wanting more time to rest, or more quality time with a loved one. It might be wanting you to take a risk, or to trust in your creative potential. Whatever it has to share, trust in its wisdom.

When you have finished listening to this part and the practice feels complete, offer it deep gratitude for its willingness to confide in you.

Furthering connection through curiosity

As we learn to practice inner curiosity, we become curious about the world around us, too—and vice versa. Simply put, curiosity is a soulful way of living that extends openness to and interest in furthering connection. It requires being non-judgmental and prioritizing listening over problem-solving. Curiosity does not mean that we do not act; it simply means we create space for our actions to be informed by others' needs, desires, interests, and skills. Curiosity invites partnership and reciprocity rather than a "savior complex" that intends to fix things without inviting others in. Notice that curiosity builds on the elements of practice that we have discussed in *settling* and *acknowledging*. These first two ground us in a sacred presence and help us notice what is real about our experience. In many ways, the movement of acknowledging assumes a certain openness that is also present in curiosity. Once we have found ways to be grounded and safe enough in our experience, then we can become more curious about our personal experiences and those of our children.

Curiosity has been a saving grace in our intercultural and interracial marriage. We have had many arguments that would have led to further disconnect if not for the power of curiosity. Practicing curiosity has not been easy, because so often we are convinced that we are right and that we are justified in our "rightness." One example of this has to do with the power of language. Communication is so important in any relationship, but culturally speaking, we are all taught to communicate and use language in vastly different ways. In our case, we had to learn that we each were taught totally different styles of communication when it came to being direct or indirect with our feelings. One of us was taught that being indirect was more polite, as it sought to avoid publicly shaming the other person. The other was taught that if you are not direct in communication, then you are not being honest. While we often felt the pain points of how we misunderstood each other, we were not entirely conscious of just how different our use of language was until we reached a breaking point and sought help from others.

So how were we to resolve this divide? In our case, we sought support to learn a more contemplative style of communication. And, as you probably guessed, the contemplative style included learning to rely on curiosity about our internal selves and about each other. Now when we experience misunderstanding or disconnect, we have tools, such as the curiosity practice, to help us become more aware of how our internal parts have been activated and what it is they are longing for. We also have learned to offer each other listening space where we can allow the other person to share fully and then reflect back on what we have heard. This approach helps us listen with compassion to one another rather than centering our own needs first. While we could have just left the arguments assuming that the other person was wrong and rude, we are grateful that curiosity gave us another option. We learned to realize that neither of us sees the whole picture. In fact, we need each other to enrich our experience.

Being curious also admits that, in everything we encounter, there is hidden wisdom to discover even if it does not initially seem so. For example, we've experienced multiple moments where one of our children has had a tantrum in a store because they were not allowed to get something they had asked for. Early on, we often met these tantrums with harsh judgment and the assumption that our child was seeking to manipulate the situation. We came to realize we only held these beliefs because there were adults in our childhood who had said these things to us. As we grew as parents, we began to see how each tantrum was a natural response to feeling anger—often a response to feeling discounted and not cherished. In this sense, a tantrum is not really about getting something at the store but more about how we can show our children that their experiences matter deeply to us. The answer is not to give them what they want all the time but to assure them we love and cherish them unconditionally. Furthermore, anger is not something to bury or shy away from. It is an important experience to cultivate because it helps us understand where our boundaries and limits need to be set. Rather than telling our children to simply obey us because we said so, curiosity becomes an opportunity to explore with our children their own inner worlds and what their desires are. While this is not always a smooth ride in the moment, over the long haul it helps our children develop trust in their own embodied experience.

We are inviting a posture of curiosity toward our children to better understand what is happening *within* them. When we are curious, it benefits us as their caregivers to be more sensitive in how we communicate. It also has even more benefits for the child to understand their own bodily experience. Extending curiosity to them does not mean that they will get everything they want. Rather, it is a way of being in a deep relationship with each other as we all learn to navigate life's changing terrain.

Curiosity and mutuality

In the Christian contemplative tradition, the practice of curiosity is all about letting life speak and be understood on its own terms. The spiritually wise person is not the one who knows all the answers and tells others what to do with certainties and solutions, but rather the person in whose presence others come to a greater self-awareness and self-compassion. It requires that we learn how to hold space, to prevent patterns of problem-solving or rushing to a conclusion that will make the discomfort stop. While curiosity can look like asking questions, it can also look like stillness. Rather than saying, "Here's what needs to happen," an inner posture of curiosity asks, "Is there something more I'm not seeing?" When we learn to trust the Divine in our moments of uncertainty, we find that there are many more creative options available to us.

Curiosity also fosters mutuality with our children and communicates to them that their experience is valuable. It tells them that we are willing to listen and even learn from them. A great place to start, however, is by first practicing curiosity within our own experiences. We've learned to ask ourselves often, "I wonder why I'm feeling this way," and in turn, we are more able to ask our child, "I'm wondering why you have tears," or "I'm wondering why you are yelling." This genuine curiosity provides our children an opportunity to honor their personal agency. For far too long, the dominant culture has assumed that children are blank slates who must be trained. When a parent practices loving curiosity with a child, at any age, there is much that can be learned from how the child perceives the world. Practicing curiosity with our children communicates to them that they are fully human and worthy of being listened to.

In the Scriptures, Jesus respects the agency of others. Jesus does not impose belief on others or take others to places they do not want to go. Take, for example, the rich young ruler who inquires after eternal life. "What good deed must I do to have eternal life?" he asks. Jesus replies that if the man wants to grow in maturity, he will have to give away all that he has. When the young ruler does not do as Jesus instructs, Jesus lets him be. Even in the cases where healing transpires, Jesus says it is due to the faith (or courage of heart) of the person who was healed. In other words, relational wholeness is a two-way street. It requires consent and trust. Parenthood requires this two-way interaction, too. At best, we model an active trust in God when we choose to embrace and enjoy the (sometimes messy) process of our lives. The same goes for our children.

Wholeness is not about working everything out so that life goes according to our plans, but about how we lean into life with a quiet confidence, one that knows we are all in this together and we are not alone in our questions and joys. We will find that our life is enriched by the perspectives and dreams of one another, and together we will begin to see the beauty and importance of each person.

Helping our children practice curiosity

According to parenting experts, an ideal time to connect to your child is at night before they fall asleep.[6] We know too well how challenging nighttime routines can be for tired parents. When we feel drained from the day, it seems as though our children tap into an extra reserve of energy and grow fixated on their next adventure—making patience feel unattainable. However, with the intention of fostering connection, nighttime rituals can become a meaningful practice at home for the entire family.

It's important to be flexible and maintain a posture of exploration as you discover what methods will work at any given moment with your children. Rather than imposing the nighttime routine on our children, we are discovering how to make the nighttime routine a practice for the whole family. These days, we all choose pajamas at the same time and show one another which pajamas we've chosen for the night (our little ones love to make their own choices!). When our children refuse to brush their teeth—it happens—we grab our toothbrushes and create a game or imaginative scenario with them so that toothbrushing becomes a playful family event. We notice a greater sense of connection and engagement when they feel we are joining them in life rather than imposing our will on them.

One particular night, after everyone had washed up, we invited our children to our room, and we all sat on the bed together. We invited each child, in the middle of their squeals, shouts, and giggles, to share one moment of the day that was interesting or surprising to them. One of our kids shared happily. Meanwhile, another expressed frustration on their face, making it very clear that they were upset. Rather than assuming the worst and scolding our child for not engaging, we decided to respond with curiosity. I (Aizaiah) asked, "We can see that you're feeling upset and we're wondering why. Can you share why you feel this way?" After a few seconds of thought, our child replied, "Because I want to watch a show instead!"

"It makes sense that you feel frustrated," I said, "because you would rather be watching a show instead." We paused and held the space in silence for a few more seconds in an attempt not to rush to any solutions. Then I said, "Right now we are sharing about our day and tomorrow we will have a chance to watch a show. Let's hear what your sibling wants to share next."

As the other siblings continued to share about their day, we filled the space with more questions and curiosity. "Who did you play that with?" we asked. "How did that make you feel?" "What animal did you see?" "Wow, that's amazing, do you think I can try that too?" While the conversation continued playfully, our frustrated child remained quiet (with a few eye rolls), and when it was their turn to share, they understandably did not feel ready.

Since our early years of parenting, we have been intentional about noticing what specific actions help each of our children feel loved and connected. Each child is dynamic and unique and often requires a different kind of action to feel seen and loved. With this particular child, who was frustrated, we knew that offering sincere compliments and naming specific moments from the day when we had seen our child show kindness, creativity, and compassion would help them feel how much we care. "I noticed when you helped your younger brother put his shoes on today," Neddy said. "That was so kind of you! It felt really special to see that." As we shared a few more affirmations, our frustrated child slowly turned their face toward ours, looked into our eyes, and smiled softly. When we finished sharing, our child leaned in for a hug, and we held their embrace. Our willingness to be curious had given us the ability to choose a different way. Rather than scolding our child for not participating in the family conversation, we were able to attune to our child's inner experience and offer them another path for connection.

The practice of curiosity in daily life models to our children how to live each day with an inner posture of openness and receptivity. Curiosity powerfully opens us up to learn and see our children anew. And when we are curious to know our children more deeply, we cultivate an attitude of respect for their inner worlds and open ourselves up to learning from and with them. While this can be awkward at first (it certainly was for us!), it can be a much more spacious way to parent because it does not require us to be perfect or to have everything figured out. Instead, we can find our way together with our children.

Other ways to practice curiosity

Reflective listening

This practice invites you to listen with more presence and with an inner posture of openness and curiosity. When your child is speaking to you, simply repeat, or "reflect," back to them what you heard them say. For example, it can look something like this:

Child: I hate this toy!
Parent: You hate the toy?
Child: Yes!
Parent: Can you tell me more?
Child: It's not working right.
Parent: Oh, it's not working right. That must feel difficult.

Reflective listening helps the other person know that they are genuinely being heard. It also can help parents not to assume, impose, or immediately offer their child a solution. Oftentimes, our children feel more connected and empowered when we are willing to simply be a listening presence as they process aloud with us. If we are patient enough, we can help our children feel our support as they process their experiences. Our compassionate curiosity can help them learn how to imagine and develop new ideas to respond to their situation.

Younger children often communicate loudly with actions rather than words. If your young child throws something, for example, you can reflect back to them what you noticed. You might say something like, "I noticed you threw your toy really hard on the ground. How are you feeling?" Then, be open to hearing their response.

Explore wonder

Whether you are gazing at the night sky, walking on a busy street, or playing at home, practice asking your child what they wonder about. (It is best to do this activity when your child is not distracted by something.) You can simply ask, "Is there anything you're wondering about?" and be open to hearing whatever they might say. If they do not respond, you can share with them some of your wonderings, and you will probably inspire them to wonder more deeply.

The art of wondering and asking questions takes practice, and when we invite our children to share their wonderings and questions with us every day, we help them cultivate this skill. Remember to always affirm your child's questions so they feel empowered in their curiosity and thank them for sharing their questions with you. You do not always have to have an answer. In fact, it's better not to! It's okay to let your children know that you don't have all the answers and perhaps together you can explore their wonderings more deeply.

Curious observation

Young children are masters at imaginative play. Whenever your children are playing, bring your full attention to them and simply notice and observe how they are engaging in their play. What makes them smile? What questions come up for them? What curiosities does your child convey?

When our eighteen-month-old wants to go for a walk, for example, we try to practice curiosity by closely following his lead and observing his natural inclination to explore. He notices the smallest things like the single blade of grass, the tiny bug, the sticks, and the bark of the trees. When we allow ourselves to fully participate in the walk through the lens of our toddler, we are more inclined to experience the gift of curiosity, wonder, and adventure.

Compassionate questions

Here are some examples of questions or phrases that can help you engage in compassionate curiosity with your child.

"I heard you say . . . Did I hear that correctly?"

"That seems really hard. How did that make you feel?"

"Thank you for sharing that with me. Is there anything else you want to share?"

"What can I do to support you?"

5

Restore

A soft answer turns away wrath. . . .
—Proverbs 15:1a

In today's world, it is widely believed that freedom is about being able to make a choice. We often hear, "Do what makes you happy." In a hyper-individualistic society, we are taught that if everyone pursues happiness for themselves, then we should all be okay. But, especially in the United States, there are many indicators that our society, which claims to prioritize the "pursuit of happiness," is out of alignment. Poverty, mental illness, and injustices have continued to rise, perpetuated by systems and structures that prioritize our lives as individuals rather than as interdependent human beings. We are told that if another person is suffering, it is a personal problem and is probably due to some moral fault or lack of faith. We know this is far from reality. While the choices we make in life do influence what happens, many other factors make life easier or harder to navigate because of our social location (these factors include things like race and ethnicity, language of origin, religious identity, disability, social class, and many more).[1]

Each aspect of our identity that is not part of the "norm" makes it more difficult to access resources, to be selected for opportunities, and to succeed. It is not that those with privileges have *easy* lives, it is simply that those who are not privileged experience more *obstacles* to success. And what do we learn from a society that values and privileges certain bodies over others yet tells us that it is all about merit, individual choice, and one's effort? Vinay Gupta, a digital innovator and philosopher, says that this mentality leads us toward becoming a "monster factory" where we produce monsters who do not care for our neighbor in need.[2] An overly individualistic approach perpetuates disconnect and disparity.

What if freedom is not the same as being able to do whatever you want? When we look at the book of Genesis, we see that God was not primarily concerned with individual choice when interrogating Cain after his brother Abel's murder. What if God is asking us the same question he asked Cain in Genesis 4:9: *Where is your sibling?* What if freedom is more about responding to life from the depths of one's true self, the deepest dimension of one's experience, and a way of living that honors self, others, and the whole? Scholar and priest Raimon Panikkar writes, "The prerogative of human freedom is not limited to the choice between given possibilities; it is not the power, either, to do or to make just anything, but to make oneself *oneself*."[3] Freedom is truly about being (and becoming) all that we are.

The reality, though, is that we often fail at this. We have to learn how to make amends, reconcile, and restore relationships that have been broken. The apostle Paul goes so far as to say that we have been given the "ministry of reconciliation" (2 Corinthians 5:18). Reconciliation is about bringing back together that which has been torn apart. In a world where we are all encouraged to do life on our own, without others, we are called to reconcile and repair instead. We believe this work begins at home with our children.

The power of loving repair

Children who have siblings often feel some version of the following: "I am so angry! Why do they always do this to me?" Some version of this sentiment is common in our household, at least. And these moments are often the hardest when we are in what we describe as the "graveyard" hour; when we are in the middle of preparing dinner and feeling a mixture of hunger and exhaustion.

In month three of the Covid lockdowns, we were already sleep-deprived as we struggled to find a sense of balance amid the arrival of our third child, who had just celebrated his first month of life. We had recently moved, and in that short time had not yet made many friendships. We felt alone, overwhelmed, and often frustrated. So, when our oldest child expressed frustration about her siblings during the infamous graveyard hour, instead of responding with love, connection, and compassion, we scolded her. "Just forget about it and leave it alone!" we said. "You are only making things worse by allowing your sibling to make you upset!"

Both of us knew immediately that was a horrible reply to a child who was rightfully upset, but we did not have the fortitude to respond lovingly. Instead, we dismissed and denied her anger—what some might call gaslighting. Of course, this only made matters worse, and she burst into tears. And then the self-critical voices piped up within: "How could you say that to her?" "How could you think you are a spiritual leader when you cannot even love your own daughter?" "Your child would be better off without you!" Our daughter's reaction catapulted us inward and took us down a path of internal self-loathing, disconnect, and frustration, inevitably leading to shame.

Shame can be a vicious cycle. Especially when you are sincerely longing to live differently than the status quo and act in wholesome, compassionate ways. During the pandemic, the two of us agreed we needed support in order to learn how to navigate the emotional demands and challenges of parenting. We met with psychospiritual practitioners and enrolled in spiritual direction training, which we pursued for several years. These experiences revealed that we could parent differently than what was modeled to us. Both of us are also the eldest child in our families, a role that strongly shaped us to crave success. We often felt pressure and a sense of responsibility to always perform and do the right thing, especially as parents. We have since realized the weight that comes with being the "oldest" and how those expectations did not teach us to be the kind of parents who could promote spiritual wholeness. While our desire to parent well came from a noble place, it was misguided. It often meant our first response to anger from our children was not grace or curiosity toward them but shame, self-criticism, and an insistence that they "do better."

As mentioned in the previous chapter on curiosity, noticing our inner critical voices, or "parts," is a large step toward developing self-awareness. Neuroscientist Dan Siegel discusses the importance of our inner critical voices, which arise from millions of years of evolution (quite miraculous!). In fact, the internal voices that identify perceived threats kept our ancient ancestors alive and on the hunt for food. But while our inner voices were once critical for survival, they might need updating so they do not have free rein to guide every decision of our day. Siegel admits these inner voices can often feel like inner dictators. "The first step is only to become aware that you have an inner [critical] voice—that's it," he says. "Then, recognize it may actually be driven by some unmet need and learn to engage with it through questions and perhaps even gratitude."[4] In other words, there is a way out of the shame cycle and into a mercy cycle.

While our critical interior voices may seem to hinder us from our goals, nothing in our spiritual lives is a quick fix. In fact, we have come to look at these challenges as invitations rather than obstacles for further healing and connection. When our inner voice says we are not patient enough or loving enough to treat our children with the respect they deserve, we can learn to notice this inner voice with curiosity. As we notice, we can begin to compassionately learn and understand where this voice comes from and what our true needs are. By opening to our fears and struggles, we have learned to accept that parenting is a long road filled with highs and lows, successes and failures. Our only task is to engage it with humility and deep mercy.

A restoring practice: Ask your sacred source to invite you to restoration

This practice is an act of faith, trusting that the Divine will reveal, at the right time, how to respond to your situation in love so that you will feel a sense of deepened connection. As you engage in this practice, it is important to hold an inner posture of stillness so that you are more able to notice what might be revealed to you. An inner posture of stillness does not require your body to be still—although we encourage you to try! You can practice this while on a walk, while drawing, humming, singing, chanting, writing, or even dancing. What is important is that you open your mind, heart, and body to be deeply aware of and attuned to your inner world.

Begin by inviting your sacred source to accompany you as you reflect on a recent or current challenging situation. Take your time as you deeply reflect on your challenging experience and notice what parts within yourself are activated.

Then, ask the Divine, or your sacred source, to reveal how you might restore right relationship with someone. Hold an inner posture of stillness as you wait and listen, noticing what the Divine might reveal to you.

Perhaps your invitation is to initiate an honest conversation with someone or to identify a boundary that is necessary for your well-being. Perhaps, it is to offer an apology to someone you hurt or to invite someone to share a meal with you. Perhaps, your invitation is to offer yourself daily affirmations or to let go of something that no longer serves you. Perhaps, it is to reconnect with nature and spend more time caring for animals or plants. Trust in your inner wisdom, which flows from the Divine, and be open to receive your divine invitation of restoration.

When you feel the practice is complete, offer gratitude to your sacred source for lovingly accompanying you in this challenging experience.

Accessing mercy

Where shall we find such depths of mercy that enable us to move toward restoration? And how do we find this in moments that seem almost impossible to access? Contemporary Christian contemplative teacher James Finley writes that true wisdom is "to say that there is no refuge from suffering, that there's no place so innocent, there's no place so pure, there's no place so well ordered, there's no place so controlled that is free from suffering." Suffering, writes Finley, "can, and eventually, will find you." Yet love undoes suffering. As Finley writes, "Suffering has no refuge from a deathless love that permeates the suffering unexplainably and all pervasively in all directions."[5]

While this may not seem comforting at first, somehow, mysteriously, the Divine interacts with us through mercy and compassion amid our frailties and failings rather than through judgment and contempt. In Hebrews 4:14–16, the letter writer speaks of the great high priest, Jesus, "who has passed through the heavens." The writer continues: "We do not have a high priest who is unable to sympathize with our weaknesses, but we have one who in every respect has been tested as we are, yet without sin." In Christ, we have a model of redemption and reconciliation. This does not mean that we are excused from any wrongs we commit. Instead, it means that the Divine grants us grace to perceive when we have fallen short and be empowered to confront our shortcomings with courage, to learn humility, and to make amends where and when necessary.

Yet we all know that it is much easier to talk about making amends than to actually *make* amends. One of the scariest and hardest things to do is to vulnerably admit our flaws and mistakes. We fear that when we acknowledge our own shortcomings, we will be exposed, and this may result in severe judgment and ultimately rejection. Although we have good intentions, you can see, our challenge is overcoming fear. We want to be connected to others. We want to feel acceptance and affirmation. And we also want to stay as far away as we can from the possibility of anything negative happening. But if we do not acknowledge our mistakes, we dehumanize ourselves (and live under a façade of piety, modeling to our children the illusion of perfectionism). In so doing, we prevent true love from being realized. True love is received not through the doors of perfect behavior but in the cracks of our mistakes. In other words, true love is true only because it is not earned. It is fully realized in the midst of our frailties.

In Romans 5:20–21 (NIV), the apostle Paul declares, "The law was brought in so that the trespass might increase. But where sin increased, grace increased all the more, so that, just as sin reigned in death, so also grace might reign. . . ." Later in 2 Corinthians 12:9, Christ tells us, "My grace is sufficient for you, for power is made perfect in weakness." These scriptural texts invite us to experience a deepening of grace in and through our weaknesses and shortcomings.

Through many challenges, we too have learned that parenting presents many opportunities to better understand these mysterious but liberating truths. Of course, we should do everything we can to respond with love and compassion in every moment, and obviously, we are deeply saddened when we inadvertently hurt or harm others due to our imperfections, but our imperfections do not have to be the end of the story. In fact, they can be a profound reminder of the importance of going within and going deeper in our own spiritual experience. For if we are going to make amends with others, it requires first that we confront the suffering within. It is only from here that we can extend compassion outward to others.

Practicing compassion within

Compassion is one of the most profound forces that leads to restorative action. We are fortunate to have been trained in a contemporary compassion practice created by contemplative practitioners Frank Rogers Jr., Andrew Dreitcer, and Mark Yaconelli. Each of these individuals has been trained and shaped by Christian contemplative spirituality as scholar-practitioners and also in the power of liberative storytelling. Their compassion practice is often taught through stories of transformation. It includes six steps, helpfully identified via the acronym PULSE: paying attention (contemplative awareness); understanding emphatically (empathetic care); loving with connection (all-accepting presence); sensing the sacredness (spiritual expansiveness); and embodying new life (desire for flourishing).[6] Our own SACRED practice has been largely inspired by the PULSE practice (many contemplative practices involve acronyms to help people remember the interconnected movements). Practicing the PULSE steps enables compassion to naturally flow to self and the world. It is a way of engaging life with tenderness rather than fear, judgment, or suppression. This practice is best done in community, where we find support and encouragement from others to keep going on the journey when it feels like too much to bear alone.

After our daughter's outburst of anger, we finished dinner, put the kids to bed, and took a moment to pause and take our own pulse.

"I can't believe I talked to our daughter that way. Sometimes it just feels like too much." Those are the words that I (Aizaiah) confessed aloud to Neddy. Taking our own pulse revealed the weariness we both were carrying and the desire to take some much-needed time for rest and renewal. We agreed that we both could support each other by allowing the other some alone time the next day to go outside and simply be in nature.

The next day, once all the kids were dropped off at daycare and school, I took a morning walk to reflect on the night before. I noticed the warm sun caress my face, the gentle motion of the tree branches, and the sounds of dogs barking and birds singing. In that moment, what I felt I needed most was to simply sit down, bask in the sun, and listen to the sound of water from a nearby stream.

Nature can be powerfully restorative. When we are surrounded by nature, we feel a sense of presence that is non-impositional, dynamic, and spacious. This experience can even offer deep cleansing of our spiritual life. In nature, we are reminded of all the self-imposed expectations that plague us, and eventually, we can sense the call to gently let them go, allowing them to flow out of us in the same way that life is constantly flowing. When we do this, we can often feel a lightness and generativity that can empower us to return to our lives with ease and a calm confidence.

My time in nature was rejuvenating and helped me find my sense of ease and calm. Later that day when the children were home from school, I asked our eldest if she would join me for a short walk together. I spent the first few moments just noticing the trees, the flowers, and the sky with her, waiting patiently to discern if there might be an opening to return to the incident from the night before. After we had spent some time laughing, telling each other silly stories, and enjoying the sunshine, I turned toward her and said, "Do you remember yesterday when you were upset with your sibling, and I told you that it was your fault?"

"Yes," she replied. Her voice was heavy.

I admitted my error. "Mom and I have been thinking about that, and you should know that our behavior was wrong. We were really tired yesterday, and there is no excuse because it was not true. We are sorry."

"Wait, so you did something wrong?"

"Yes. And it makes sense that you felt upset because your sibling was not listening to you. Is that right?"

She opened up. "Well yes, sometimes I feel like nobody is listening to what I feel. I just wish sometimes that my sibling would understand me." I was touched by her transparency.

"That makes a lot of sense," I said. "Perhaps when we go back inside, we can talk with your sibling, let them know how you felt, and we can ask if they can do something different next time." She nodded, exchanged a hug with me, and released a huge sigh.

Practicing compassion to our children

It is important to remember that making amends is much more than saying sorry. It is a commitment to learn from our mistakes and do our best to act differently. Our apology is not complete until we are willing to change how we will relate moving forward. Practicing restorative connection is a lifelong skill that we are called to cultivate, one day and one mistake at a time.

Practicing restoration may not always come naturally or easily. Many times, it will seem to fall flat. Yet, what is most important is that we remain willing, open, and sincere. As contemplative Thomas Merton often said, "A little sincerity with God goes a long way."[7] The same is true with our human relationships. If we can truly show the sincerity of our own heart, it can open up the depths within another. And through our experiences of disconnection, we can learn to lean in and attempt repair—especially if our children are also open and ready. It is important not to force or impose repair on our children. Instead, we should invite them to it according to their openness and personality. Oftentimes, that will require taking more time to validate and understand their experience before they are ready to make amends.

It is not about how we fail as parents but how we choose to respond and move forward. Parenting compassionately requires that we must first offer compassion to ourselves before we can repair with our children. Often this journey may include feelings of shame, doubt, regret, or self-judgment, but it does not have to end with that. We can return again and again to the mercies that are new every morning and are present in every failure. As Lamentations 3:22–23 attests, "The steadfast love of the LORD never ceases, his mercies never come to an end; they are new every morning; great is your faithfulness."

Helping our children practice restorative action

When we feel exhausted, it can be easy to act from a place of rigidity. Often this is our false belief that we will only be okay if particular actions occur. As children, we each learned to survive in our families by acting in particular ways to receive approval and acceptance. Without critical and contemplative reflection, those patterns continue into our adulthood. Over time, however, our growing experiences with the unconditional love and positive regard of the Divine have influenced the way we interact with our children. When we have abided in this interior posture, we've learned that we have more options in a given moment. There are in fact, multiple ways we can navigate an encounter. This awareness stems from the harmony within ourselves and with our children.

We call this a posture of *nonreactivity* because it recognizes that there are ways to respond in life other than out of our immediate reaction. Nonreactivity moves beyond the rigidity we internalized as children. It is not the same as passivity. Nonreactivity means we respond from a wider field that includes our personal experience and those we love, but in a more openhearted and compassionate way.

When a new school year began, not surprisingly, the change in our daily routine caused challenging emotions for our younger children. The morning routine was getting difficult. As the days went by, our two younger children continued to express that they didn't want to go to school. We practiced being curious with them to explore why they didn't want to go, empathized with their feelings, and invited them to share ideas on what could make school feel more manageable.

The two of us also talked about how we could nurture our home life to feel more grounded and restful for our children. Together, we decided to take a close look at the hours in our day and integrate a daily rhythm that would leave room for more spacious transitions in and out of the home, and support time for rest, mealtimes, and play. We experimented for a couple of weeks with this new rhythm and found a few key factors to be of great help.

First, we wanted to help our children wake up slowly and not at the last minute, so they didn't feel rushed. We set the alarm a little earlier than usual and have experienced the benefits of greeting our children in the morning with our full attention and not feeling rushed to get ready. We often greet our children with a "Good morning!" and offer them a hug if they would like one. We also are intentional not to be distracted on our phones. Instead, we offer our full attention to our children as they wake up and head to the table for breakfast. Contemplative parenting reminds us to be present in life as it unfolds, and starting our day with full presence has proven to help our home feel more loving and grounded as we begin our day.

Second, we noticed that spaciousness supports a smooth transition from after school to heading back home. When we pick up our children (we trade on and off depending on our schedules), we don't immediately ask them questions about their day. We simply greet them with a smile, offer a hug, and let them take the lead on what they want to share. Our presence offers them support to help them transition—at their pace—to the next part of their day. We've also noticed how much more grounded our kids feel when they are not being rushed to the next thing. Because of this, we aim to schedule after-school activities or appointments with enough time for our kids to transition without feeling hurried or rushed. We also keep water or snacks easily available for them in the car and at home to help them practice noticing and taking care of their body if they feel hungry or thirsty.

When we arrive home from school, our children often ask right away if they can watch television. It makes sense that after a long day of learning new things, our kids simply want to relax and watch something entertaining! However, we have noticed that in our home, television feels more like an escape and does not usually help any of us feel more seen or grounded once the show is over.[8] Because cultivating connection within ourselves and with one another is a value we've learned through contemplative parenting, we've chosen to take about half an hour to simply be together after the school day ends. This usually looks like eating snacks, talking together, and providing space for our children to process whatever may be coming up for them. Sometimes they grab a toy or some art supplies and we encourage them to simply engage in whatever play or creative activity feels right as they settle back into the home. We've noticed that having this intentional time after school helps us all feel more grounded as we transition back into homelife together.

We also practice engaging in family conversations about what our day will look like. We have this conversation in the morning and usually again after school to help our children feel more secure and confident about what the day will bring. We invite our kids to join us as we create a family plan, and we literally write it out on paper for our kids to see it for themselves. It isn't always a smooth conversation! Our kids all have different preferences on what we should do. However, our intention is to model and practice giving everyone a chance to share their ideas, and then we determine together how our plan can best support each other's needs. We love how this enables us to demonstrate a "both-and" approach to family, meaning we can practice honoring individual needs and honoring the whole. There is no clear-cut way to do this, and it requires discernment, love, patience, and deep listening. But with consistent practice, we can develop greater capacity to support the needs of one another.

Finally, we started a family ritual at bedtime that helps our children experience inner connection as they prepare to rest. Our children are at ages where they still appreciate being tucked into bed by a parent. After we tuck them in, we offer them an opportunity to say a prayer to God just to share what is in their heart. If they don't feel ready to share, that is okay. We remain consistent in the invitation. We end by reciting a short Spanish prayer from Psalms 4:8 that was passed on to us from Neddy's family. What we've noticed is that as our children grow older and become used to this bedtime ritual, they feel more comfortable and willing to share what they are experiencing within, and there is a greater sense of trust and peace.

We recognize the great diversity of home life, work schedules, and rhythms, and we understand life is constantly changing. We also anticipate that our own rhythms will drastically shift as our kids get older. We offer this as an invitation to consider how restoration might unfold through the daily practice of being present to one another, especially during moments of transition throughout the day. Because, when children feel seen and cared for by their parent or caregiver, their sense of inner safety and confidence grows.

Other ways to practice restorative action

Foster creativity and ideation

Notice opportune moments to ask your child what ideas *they* might have to resolve a situation. Whether during playtime, recreation time, chore time, or homework time, practice frequently asking your child what ideas they have to problem-solve. If your child is upset because a toy or gadget is not working, for example, consider asking them what ideas they have to make their situation better. Or if your child had a hard time with a friend at school, consider asking what ideas they have to help restore the relationship. When your child shares their ideas, reflect back to them what you heard, and affirm their creative thinking.

For children who do not communicate verbally, notice their body cues. Are they pointing? Imitating sounds? Looking somewhere specific? A daily practice of inquiring and listening to what our children have to offer is a spiritual practice developing our inner capacity to remain tender in love. This practice also empowers our children to reconnect to themselves and gain confidence in their creative abilities.

Both-and mantras

Both-and mantras can be a powerful practice to cultivate capacity to hold multiplicity and even polarities within ourselves.[9] Below are some examples of both-and mantras that can bring a sense of grounding in a challenging situation. Feel free to explore and create your own both-and mantras that feel right to you and your children in any given moment.

"Yes, I feel sad, and I am filled with love."

"Yes, I feel hurt, and I have the power to make this right."

"Yes, I feel alone, and God is with me to give me strength."

Restore through play

Oftentimes, talking through a difficult emotion is not effective or developmentally appropriate for young children. The emotion feels too large and intense, flooding their nervous system. To help create a sense of grounding during an emotionally charged encounter, consider pausing and engaging in a conversation of repair with your child through play.

For example, if you just had a heated conversation with your child where both of you felt frustration, give yourself permission to pause, ground yourself, and reset. When the next opportunity arises to engage with your child, you can use toys, dolls, or stuffed animals to model a conversation of repair. The following dialogue reflects a moment we had with our eight-year-old while playing with stuffed animals and using the stuffed animals to represent our repairing conversation.

Parent: I had a big emotion and spoke to you in an unkind way. I'm sorry I did that.

Child: Thank you for saying sorry. I feel sad when you speak in a mean way.

Parent: Thank you for sharing that with me. It makes sense that you felt sad when I spoke to you in a mean way. I love you and I want to practice speaking kind to you. How does that sound?

Child: Good.

Parent: That sounds good to me too.

Create a time map

This practice invites you to reflect at the end of each day and imagine how tomorrow will be.[10] As you consider tomorrow, write down a visual time map of how you will engage the day. The time map can be simple or as visually creative as you desire it to be. Consider dividing your day into three-hour blocks, and in each block of time, write down what activity or activities you will do. Be sure to write in every block of time from the hour you wake up to when you go to sleep. The purpose of this practice is to help you feel free of having to keep a mental list of what needs to be done so you can engage in each daily activity with more presence.

In our home, we post a weekly time map in the kitchen as a daily reminder of how we intend to engage our days. This practice can help us restore our relationship with time if we feel stressed, hurried, or overburdened. And it fosters deeper familial connection as we engage our days with more presence and less mental distractions.

6
Enjoy

You show me the path of life. In your presence there is fullness of joy. . . .
—Psalm 16:11

We'll be honest. Sometimes joy feels disingenuous. Things happen in our lives that are just sorrowful and tragic. And we never wish to diminish or romanticize our difficult human experiences. We've often pondered, though, how joy can truly show up in our lives in the midst of so much pain, violence, and suffering.

Archbishop Desmond Tutu was an anti-apartheid leader and contemplative in South Africa who was jailed for his justice work. "Discovering more joy does not save us from the inevitability of hardship and heartbreak," he writes. "In fact, we may cry more easily, but we will laugh more easily too. Perhaps we are just more alive. Yet as we discover more joy, we can face suffering in a way that ennobles rather than embitters."[1] According to Tutu, enjoyment of life is not merely about embracing the good. Joy is a practice of intentionally returning to humility and gratitude before God. And joy is closely connected to rest when we learn to relax into our experience as we abide in God. One of the most ancient Christian contemplatives, St. Augustine, writes, "You have made us for yourself O Lord and our heart is restless until it rests in you."[2] Joy, then, is truly countercultural because it flows from our willingness to experience life with a greater awareness that God is at work and that we can ultimately rest in and celebrate this enduring promise.

Practicing joy, however, can be extremely difficult due to the realities of life in a consumerist society. We often hear parents say something like, "I can't wait until my baby crawls." Or "I can't wait until my baby can talk," or whatever else it might be. When we were first-time parents, we felt this way, too, and at times we would look forward to what our baby would do next. There is nothing *wrong* with futurist thinking, yet the dominant culture in North American society is designed to make us feel that we are missing something now and we need to go out and find or acquire what we do not yet possess. The messaging from corporations and company executives often communicates that we are lacking, and we need something external to achieve fulfillment and be more content. Commercials and advertisements inundate us with information on what products or services are best and most personalized for us. But our needs cannot be satisfied with products or materialistic "goods" or professional achievements. From a contemplative perspective, true enjoyment comes when we are wholly given to Love. In fact, when more and more goods are purchased, it often leads to clutter: physical clutter, mental clutter, and soul clutter. Some may say that you can always donate what you no longer need, which is true. However, continually donating or throwing away items leads to garbage clutter on the earth. And we know that we live humbly at the mercy of the natural systems of the planet. If we overconsume and harm the land, the earth will respond and cry out for justice (Luke 19:40; Romans 8:22).

In our mega-information age, it is too easy to fill our thoughts with an "ask Google or Siri." We are trained to look at social media, email, news, or television during any quiet moment. And we recognize that for parents, it's rare to have a quiet moment. In fact, how often when the kids are entertaining themselves, do we find ourselves looking at our phones and scrolling through more information?

We do not mean to demonize the act of looking at our phones. We know this is a way of life for many today, including us. But our intention is to bring awareness to the reality that filling our minds with more information rarely offers us the rejuvenation, satisfaction, or connection we long for. What if our ability to feel connected and renewed was always available to us deep within? While knowledge is not bad, it is empty without love. Where can we find this love?

The challenge of simply enjoying life as it is also spills into the lives of our children. Our children see and hear advertisements and messages on television, tablets, marketing mailers, and even from their peers. When we hear our children say things like "I want this toy!" or "Can you buy me this?" we are mindful to respond with understanding because we know firsthand how exciting it is to get a new toy or gadget to play with. However, we also recognize that in our North American context, our children will constantly be receiving messages that more is better.

Sacred simplicity

The good news is that we have a radical alternative. We can practice a life of sacred simplicity. Simplicity is not about living in scarcity, but about living in harmony with the one thing that matters. It is a matter of bringing our whole hearts to each moment and experiencing whatever life brings, allowing God to work within us and through us for holistic transformation. From a spiritual perspective, simplicity is a heart and mind attuned to what is most true and essential in life. We consider how our bodies are feeling, how our hearts are feeling, and what actions nurture our wholeness.

The story of Mary and Martha in the Gospels offers some guidance (Luke 10:38–42). In this story, we find that Martha is busy doing many important things for Jesus' ministry. While this is very useful and productive, Jesus is quick to point out that Mary, who is simply sitting at the feet of Jesus, has found the "better part." This story is often interpreted as a call to imitate the prayer and worshipful posture of Mary that is set apart from daily work activities and routines. Though we agree that time away is important, we want to take this story a bit deeper and reflect on the possibility that we can maintain the devotional posture that Mary exemplifies in everyday life. In other words, this story teaches us that it is not about just going away for prayer retreats (although these are good!), but about the ways we entrust each moment and action to God and allow divine love to flow through us. That is the one thing and *main* thing that Mary found—and it is always available to us. How is this so? Because love never runs out or goes away. Love is the very reality that permeates and sustains all things continuously. The challenge is learning to return to that posture and be sustained in that flow of love rather than getting caught up and preoccupied with our plans, wishes, or agendas. We call the example of Mary one of sacred simplicity.

What are some ways we can sustain our lives in this simplicity amid the mundane? For us, we believe that simplicity at home starts with connection. We often ask each other, how connected do we feel to ourselves, to one another, and to God? Are we stuck wishing that we could be somewhere else, doing something else, or having life a different way? We've found that to live in simplicity is to live each and every moment from a place of radical partnership with God and the world. In other words, our loving relationship with ourselves, God, and others is what sustains us.

In a practical sense, consider how you feel when you are at home. We find ourselves asking questions like, does our home feel spacious or cluttered? Does it feel safe or tense? Relaxed or too busy? When we bring sacred intentionality to our day, it helps us relax into the natural flow of life and be sustained. For us, intentionality is vital, but it is very different from simply making plans. Plans are not bad in and of themselves, but they can become idols in our hearts if we allow them to dictate our lives. Intentionality is different and more subtle. Intentionality tells us that our life matters, this moment matters, and what we are doing matters. Intentionality is about living with a truly discerning and present attitude rather than one that is fixed or attached to how we think things should unfold. If we can maintain this attitude toward our day and our children, we can trust that God will work through us.

A practice of simplicity at home resists dominant cultural norms that shout at us to sacrifice our today for a better tomorrow. God invites us to sacrifice our plans and agendas for the future so we can be fully present during *this* day. A practice of simplicity is therefore personal but not individualistic, as it intends to cultivate *collective* well-being. As the Cistercian Christian contemplative Mario Águilar says, "There is a direct relation between the following of God and the compassion for the poor and there is a direct connection between centering the periphery and the demands for a simpler life."[3] In other words, true simplicity is akin to doing justice in the world. It doesn't mean we are stuck trying to change reality. Rather, true simplicity sees that reality is about promoting right relationship and harmony, and in order to cultivate that in the wider world, we must first embody right relationship with ourselves. Simplicity in spiritual life is what brings "blessedness," says Raimon Panikkar. The one who lives in simplicity, he writes, "is the one who tries to swim upstream, against the current, to the origin which one supposes to be simple. God is simple."[4]

As our children grow, one of the greatest gifts we can model is how to live a life of sacred simplicity. Rather than trying to fill your calendar with extracurricular activities, notice which activities can be put on hold or perhaps let go of to help the whole family have the space they need to simply rest, play, and be. The temptation to overcommit and overconsume is strong in our consumerist culture, especially because it trains us to feel anxious about the future and worried about survival. When you feel this, lean into the words of Jesus, which tell us to trust in God and live for today (Matthew 6:34).

An enjoying practice: Savor the newfound connection experienced in your loving response

The earlier movements of the SACRED practice invited you to settle into your sacred source, acknowledge what has come up for you, be curious to learn from it, and respond restoratively. This fifth movement is about further integrating new life energy into your body and personal experience. It is easy to move quickly from one thing to the next, but this practice is about allowing yourself to savor the richness and joy of a restorative experience.

> To begin this practice, find a comfortable position where you can engage in self-reflection. Bring your awareness to your breath, and allow yourself to simply be still for about a minute, anchoring your awareness in the natural rhythm of your breath.

Then, reflect on a recent memory when you experienced deep joy or restoration of relationship with yourself, God, or another. It could be a moment when you hugged a loved one or when you took time to offer yourself care. It could be when you experienced intimacy with God or the sacred. Notice which memory comes to mind, and for the next few minutes, allow yourself to sink deeper into this memory, remembering how each of your senses was engaged.

Allow the goodness of this experience to permeate your whole being. Give yourself permission to savor joy.

Then, notice if a word, color, or image comes to mind that feels connected to this experience of joy. The image could be a body of water, a plant, an animal, or anything that will help you remember this moment. Allow the word, color, or image to be a reminder to you of the joy you felt in this experience.

When you feel ready, take a few deep breaths to help you settle back into your body and gently bring your awareness back into your physical space.

Offer yourself gratitude for giving yourself the gift of savoring restorative connection and joy.

Discernment

Parenting invites us to model and teach our children how to be self-reflective and to discern what is good and necessary for our lives. To enjoy our lives means we take time to reflect deeply. When we reflect deeply, we are able to listen to what God is speaking to us, and we can discern what actions we can take.

From the contemplative Christian perspective, there is nothing we need that we do not already have, because intimacy with the Divine is always available to us. A prominent Christian contemplative from the sixteenth century named St. Ignatius of Loyola taught a practice of discernment called the Awareness Examen (*examen* means to give careful examination). The examen is intended to "notice the presence of God in one's daily life and to live in generous response to it."[5] In this practice, a person takes time at the end of each day to reflect on where the Divine felt close or far off throughout the day. Both experiences offer us invitations to deepen our awareness of God, who is always with us and beyond us.

As parents, we are grateful for opportunities to practice the Awareness Examen, especially during the pandemic when so much felt uncertain and overwhelming. We prayed each day, "Where are you, God? How can I be more open and responsive to discern your presence with us?" And we allowed ourselves to wonder what would happen if our daily practice was to notice a life-affirming moment and savor its goodness. Even though life is full of suffering and oppression, we asked, could sacred moments be welling up around us? This discernment process enabled us to become aware of God at work in our lives even in the mundane. Especially during the pandemic, we often felt drained and depleted at the end of the day. After practicing the Awareness Examen, we found renewed joy in remembering the small moments when our children brought smiles to our faces. Moments like these refilled us with divine strength.

Discernment is not about final conclusions but about developing an ongoing personal relationship with the Divine that is sustained in joy. We are called to pause, slow down, and celebrate this one life we have been given. As we have learned to practice discernment and enjoyment in our daily lives, our kids have started to also notice. We have invited them into our daily reflection practice and find joy in practicing together even if it is brief. We simply ask our children what part of their day felt happy and what part of their day felt hard. It's amazing to see their enthusiasm as they share. We trust that even if they spend only a few minutes reflecting, they will learn to make this a way of life in time.

Helping our children enjoy

Now that our children are in school, they are experiencing more opportunities to share about their ethnic identity and background. We value teaching our children about their multiracial and multicultural identity, and we dive deep into the beauty of the traditions and cultures our families come from.

Although the multiracial population is exponentially increasing in the United States,[6] there are still instances when our children's multiracial experience feels ignored or marginalized. Our daughter, for example, has found herself to be one of the very few students in her class who is multiracial, and sometimes she feels like she is an outsider.

One day after school, she approached me (Neddy) and said, "I wish my hair was lighter."

"You wish your hair was lighter?" I asked, in a gentle voice.

"Yes," she said. "My friends are so pretty, and they don't have dark hair like me. I wish my eyes were blue too."

Touched by her honesty, I thanked her for sharing with me. "That must feel sad to wish your hair and eyes looked different," I said.

"I would be prettier if I looked like my friends."

Then I invited her to name aloud with me the hair and eye color of our extended family members, close friends, and neighbors. "What do you notice about the hair and eye color of all of these people?" I asked

Our daughter replied, "We all have different hair and eye color, even skin colors."

"That's right! When God made us, God made each of us unique, and we are each beautiful in our own unique way." I could feel our daughter's heart soften in that moment. "Are you willing to try something with me?" I asked.

"Sure,"

"Let's take turns looking in the mirror and say aloud, 'I am beautiful, and I am loved just as I am.'"

As our daughter said these words of affirmation to herself, I couldn't help but smile at the sweetness of that moment. "How does saying that to yourself make you feel?" I asked her.

"Good," she replied with a happy smile on her face.

Teaching our children to soak in feelings of joy and self-accomplishment helps them tap into what it feels like to be fully alive. As humans, it's easy to stay stuck on what feels difficult or challenging. But it's also true that we have the capacity to savor what is good and joyful and let these experiences sustain us for whatever life may bring. In every season, there are challenges, but there are also gifts and blessings we can learn to notice and savor.

Other ways to practice enjoyment

Enjoy an embrace

When your child is ready and receptive, offer them a hug and allow yourself to savor the hug for at least ten seconds. You can invite your child to count aloud with you too! Research shows the tremendous impacts of hugs—they can spark the release of the feel-good hormone oxytocin, help regulate the nervous system, and reduce stress. To deepen this practice, notice when your child naturally leans in for a hug. Hold the hug until they are ready to let go.

Feel your pulse

With your finger, find a pulse point on your body and hold your finger there for thirty or sixty seconds. As you feel your pulse, offer gratitude for all that your body does for you. Savor each heartbeat as a gift. Invite your children to find their pulse points, and practice this with them too.

Share affirmations

In a moment when there is space for attentive conversation, invite your child or children to share affirmations with you or one another. You can begin by noticing something specific from the day that you want to acknowledge and affirm in each child. For example, "I noticed when your water spilled at the table, you grabbed a napkin and cleaned it up. Thank you for caring for our home. I love and appreciate that about you!"

With four young children, the level of energy in our home is through the roof. Often the best times to engage in a conversation are when we are all at the table for a meal or when we are settling down before bed. Our hope is that you don't feel forced to create an opportune moment—instead, look for times when moments like these can arise naturally and your home feels ready for this kind of intimacy.

Digest and metabolize

After completing an activity, whether it be watching a show, scrolling on social media, playing, working, exercising, reading a book, or something else, take a moment to reflect on what you just experienced. Sit with whatever information you just received and take a few deep breaths. If possible, identify what your greatest takeaway was from your activity.

This practice can help us become more aware of how experiences impact us and connect us to the greater web of life. It can also help us appreciate and savor experiences.

Helping children digest and metabolize after activities like watching a television show, being with a friend, playing a sport, and so on, can help them develop a capacity for self-awareness. For example, after your child watches a show, you could ask them, "How are you feeling? What did you notice during the show?" Helping your child learn the practice of self-reflection empowers them to learn how to lovingly connect and relate to themselves.

Doing hard (courageous) things

Locate a common place at home where you can easily keep track of when you and your child accomplish something hard or difficult. For example, in our home, we tend to record things on the whiteboard in our kitchen. On the board or on a sheet of paper, list the names of those who want to participate, then at the end of the day (or week), reflect together on what difficult or challenging things you were able to accomplish. Add a checkmark next to each person's name for every difficult thing they accomplished.

Decide with your children how many checkmarks in total you want to earn together until you get a special celebration. For example, in our home, when we reach fifty check marks, we celebrate by doing something special together.

Welcome the day

In the morning before you dive deep into your work or daily tasks, take time to welcome the day. Face the direction of the sun either by looking through a window or by going outside. Allow the sun's warmth to touch your face. You can gently close your eyes and soak in the warmth of the sun. Savor this moment for about one minute, and then thank the sun for rising again. Children may especially enjoy practicing this together!

7

Dance

So if anyone is in Christ, there is a new creation: everything old has passed away; look, new things have come into being!

—2 Corinthians 5:17

One morning I (Aizaiah) sat down to eat breakfast alongside our eighteen-month-old son. I was enjoying the meal and decided to read a book about prayer while eating. The content was deeply engaging. It emphasized how life is all about the here and now and how it does little good to read about life—it is much better to experience it. While I was caught up enjoying the thought of living fully in the here and now, my child slammed the book shut! I was surprised and unsure why that happened. Did he need more food or water? The answer was no, so I opened my book back up and started reading again.

A few moments later, he slammed my book again! "What do you need?" I asked. He excitedly pointed outside the window at a baby squirrel who was there looking at us and enjoying its breakfast too. In an instant, I found myself learning one of the most profound lessons from my child: how to truly live in the here and now. When we do, we get to witness the unexpected that we couldn't plan for even if we tried. My child could not communicate it with words, but he taught me something at a much deeper level: life is a dance happening all around us, if we would only close our books and distractions to experience it for ourselves.

Dance brings us to the final movement of the SACRED practice. In our embodied presence, which is actively listening and responding to God, we become empowered to live creatively in each moment. We become inspired by the Spirit to dance in a unique way moment by moment and breath by breath. Here we find harmonious movement with the Divine, creating together new possibilities for today. Dancing in this sense is moving in deeper resonance with life and embodying resurrection as we live into the new thing God has for us. In this dimension of our practice, we emphasize the spontaneous actions that emerge in life rather than staying stuck in our ego-focused habits, plans, or agendas.

Dominant culture perpetuates a lack of creativity in us and in our children. Because we live in the age of entertainment, information, and consumerism, we are trained to believe that we must always fill our time with something we can consume or acquire. It takes great intention to practice pausing, connecting to our inner creativity, and developing a new possibility for the day. For many parents, hearing your children say "I'm bored" probably comes at the most difficult moments, such as when you still have work to do or tasks to finish. It isn't always easy to know how to respond. But what if we could grow to see these moments as invitations rather than roadblocks? We trust that when our children express boredom, we have an opportunity to respond with our presence supporting them by exploring their inner creativity and discovering what they can do next. The next time you hear your child say they're bored, we encourage you to invite them to consider what their body might need or what creative ideas they have about what they could do next. (For some help, see the BORED practice suggestion in the last section of this chapter.)

It can also feel challenging to tap into our own creativity as parents. Our social structures value order more than participating in what life is naturally and creatively becoming. Dominant Western Christian theology has perpetuated this desire for order by interpreting scripture to mean that God is a God who never changes and is in complete control. When we believe that God is in control of all things and never changes, how does this impact our response when life brings sudden change? Do we believe that we are to simply watch God work and not participate with God? Do we assume that change is bad and not part of the Divine's hand at work?

The call to dance is grounded in the awareness that life is creative. A major inhibitor to authentic creativity, however, is the presence of unresolved trauma. Trauma can be personal, intergenerational, or cultural. And trauma can prevent free creative expression inside of us. If we are to dance with life, it must come from a place of integration and wholeness. This is different from an expectation of perfection. Perfection requires an absence of error, whereas wholeness is about embracing the totality of our experiences and learning to approach them with unending love.

When the two of us were growing up, whenever we had questions, we were taught to quickly turn to scripture to find answers. While we value and appreciate the wisdom of the scriptures, we were not necessarily taught to use them to help us open our hearts and minds to discover what new and emergent thing God was inviting us into. We were taught instead to read things literally and not have any doubts about them.

We have found the scriptures to be much more powerful when we bring our doubts and questions to them because that is the place where radical openness emerges. The scriptures then guide us into co-creating a new possibility for our today that fosters God's love.

For minoritized communities, structural oppression inhibits space to freely dream, create, and dance. One winter evening, I (Neddy) was on a FaceTime call with my grandparents, and I asked my grandfather to share about the first time he crossed the border from México to the United States. He gazed upward as he recalled his earlier years. He was fourteen when he had to cross the Río Grande for the first time. He crossed it alone because his father sent him to find work so he could provide money for his ill mother, who desperately needed medicine. He felt terrified as he crossed the border, his body was tense and trembling. He remembered tripping and dropping his bag of clothes into the river and then desperately retrieving his bag in hopes he could save what remained of his wet clothing. When he made it to the United States, he found the work his father had arranged for him and did whatever it took to provide for his family, at the mercy of those who looked down on him as a poor young Mexican boy.

In hearing this story, we couldn't help but reflect on the courage my grandfather embodied in such a risky situation and at such a young age. Our grandparents have many more stories like these, and we've come to realize how the need to survive affected our ancestors to live a more cautious, risk-averse, and compliant life as immigrants in the United States. As a result, in our own upbringings, there was not much room to challenge the status quo. The call to "be grateful" was almost weaponized against us. The focus was on how to pursue a life of security and success rather than one of justice and solidarity with all. But what if we've reached a turning point? What if we embraced our family stories and connected to the great courage of our ancestors so that today we can use that courage to truly live free?

Dancing toward freedom

The practice of dancing, in a literal sense, allows our hearts and spirits to soften and open to receive a beautiful spiritual outpouring of love and joy. Dance is one of the most original and longstanding spiritual practices from across contemplative traditions. Dance is also a path to wholeness because it is an act of celebrating the gift of life we have been given (with all its felt contradictions). Celebration opens us up to new possibilities of deepening and expanding the love that has been there all along. In the book of 2 Samuel, King David danced as a symbol of surrender and complete joy and honor to God (and he danced fiercely, to the point of removing his clothes; 2 Samuel 6). In the dancing, there was freedom. What would happen if we gave ourselves permission to dance freely and unashamed? What would it feel like if we danced with our children? What would our children feel if they could dance freely?

One evening we were cleaning up after dinner, and as you can expect at this time of the day, we really started to feel tired. Our kids had been fighting sickness, and the extra energy required to care for little ones who were sick was finally catching up to us. As we were cleaning up, we asked our kids to please wash up for bed. Our kids continued to play and did not respond to our request. After asking a few more times and still getting no reply, we realized that our day had been busy with work and home duties, and we hadn't spent much time simply playing or connecting with one another. We asked our children once again to wash up for bed, and one of our children looked at us and loudly blurted out, "No!" We could feel frustration brewing in the room on all sides. Both of us looked at each other and took a moment to take a deep sigh.

When our children show signs of frustration, we are learning to discern the root of their behavior. We trust that our children long to be seen, and their behavior can signal an underlying need that is not being met. In this case, we were able to also recognize that our own frustration was activated, take a pause to acknowledge it, and then offer space for our children to process their felt experience. Realizing that our simple request to wash up was not sufficient for the moment, we decided to pause and sit quietly at the table next to our children. The child who blurted out "No!" looked at us with a sense of guilt and sadness. "Do you hate me?" they asked quietly.

We've noticed that sometimes when our children sense our frustration, they internalize this experience and believe it is their duty to keep their parents happy. In psychology, this is described as the phenomenon of the "adapted child." The child learns to take on behaviors to keep the family unit relatively stable.[1] Unfortunately, this behavior proves to be costly, even into adulthood, because it means a person continuously changes their behavior to please people rather than acting from their deepest and truest identity.

Our approach is to counter this by admitting when we have not been supportive of our children's holistic well-being. "We don't hate you," I (Neddy) said to our child. "We always love you in every moment, even if it feels hard. Love never goes away." Then we invited them, and their siblings, to color with us. We started drawing individual "parts maps." This coloring activity, which we learned about from

Carmen Jimenez-Pride, a clinical social worker and play therapist, allows someone to reflect on what they are feeling and experiencing.[2] We use different colors to express the different feelings or parts of us that are activated with emotions. We have noticed that this activity is very helpful for all of our children—and it can truly be for anyone since you do not have to be naturally drawn to art to try it.

After we grabbed the coloring supplies and sat next to our children at the table, we drew outlines of a human body on several pieces of paper. Then we began to color on our own paper, filling in the body outline using different colors to represent different emotions we had experienced throughout the day. After watching us color for a couple of minutes, our children grabbed their paper and crayons and began coloring in their bodies. As we colored, we modeled to them the practice of reflecting aloud what each color represented.

"This green color in my legs represents when I felt tired from picking up toys and my legs just wanted to lay down and rest," Aizaiah said.

"This pink color in my chest area represents when I felt happy that we could play outside for a little bit and enjoy the sunshine," I said next.

As we reflected out loud, one of our children said, "I'm not listening to what you're saying."

And we simply replied, "That's okay, we're just reflecting on our different emotions from the day." We knew that what we were modeling was being received, even if our child didn't want to admit it!

When we finished coloring our different parts, we watched the children color in theirs, and they began to share their reflections aloud too. "The purple in my arms is when I felt calm," one said.

"The red in my hands is when I felt angry," said another. As each child shared their different parts, the energy in the room shifted tangibly to one of calm, creativity, and connection.

One of our greatest takeaways as a family was noticing how we experience a wide variety of emotions in one day. We also noticed that we had experienced far more positive emotions than difficult ones. Oftentimes, our difficult emotions feel so large that we tend to forget about all the good moments that carried us through the day. We ended our time by remembering that even though circumstances change throughout the day, love is always present and available to us.

After about fifteen minutes of reflecting together, our children were in a much better mood and willing to help pick up whatever remaining items were left to put away. We accompanied our children to the bathroom to help them wash up for the night and tucked them into bed. The calmness of their bodies and softness in their faces showed us that they felt seen, loved, and valued and now felt ready to lie down for the night.

Sometimes, dancing looks like coloring your legs green! The power of creative expression, or what we call *dance*, can create new ways of seeing and being with one another. Creating together with our children can be a transformative act, especially for our children who do not fit or conform to society's norms. We have the Divine opportunity every day to dance anew again and again.

A dancing practice: Celebrate deep transformation

Dance is the final movement of the SACRED practice. It allows us to creatively act from a place of newfound or restored aliveness. It is a place of openness to the world as our actions flow from a place of full-heartedness, generosity, and care. Dance is profoundly spontaneous and creative. We can dance—however it looks—without any expectations for a particular outcome. It is a pure overflow of one's experience and is the returning place for the SACRED practice to begin again, finding grounding and settling in the divine flow of reality.

> To begin this practice, find a quiet space where you can reflect internally. Invite your sacred source to accompany you and take a few deep breaths to help you settle into the present moment.
>
> Next, recall a recent moment when you experienced deep love and connection. Allow this memory to sink in for a few minutes remembering how your senses were activated in that experience.
>
> Next, begin to imagine what celebration could look like as you honor the gifts granted to you in your life. What would it look like to deepen and expand the energy of the gifts you received, perhaps through a shared meal, creating art, building community, engaging in play, connecting with nature, singing a song, or offering a dance? Allow your imagination to flow freely. Notice what act of celebration feels most right to you.
>
> Offer gratitude to your sacred source for the newfound aliveness you have experienced and cherish the celebration!

Helping our children dance

Creating openness within ourselves as parents enables us to communicate with our children as creative collaborators rather than as authoritarians. We've noticed that connection is hindered when our children feel that we are imposing our agenda on them. True connection and love are experienced when we are grounded in the faith that together we can create something new. Our children can intuitively sense when we provide them with the opportunity to contribute their ideas, skills, and talents. They feel empowered, and this empowerment travels with them into other environments and public spaces. When we are speaking to our children, we want to foster a free and compassionate space for them to explore and connect to their inner wisdom.

One afternoon, we went outside as a family to get some fresh air. Our younger kids grabbed their bikes while our eldest had to settle for her scooter because she had outgrown her bike. She was making it obvious that she was disappointed. She dropped her shoulders and said in an aggravated tone that she did not want to go outside with the family.

We knew her resistance was connected to not having a bike of her own. So, we tried to show a sense of understanding. "Does it feel hard that you don't have a bike of your own?" we asked.

"Yes!" she replied.

We thanked her for sharing. "It is hard to not have your own bike while your siblings get to ride theirs," we said. "It makes sense that you feel upset. Since it's time for us to play outside, you can choose to walk or ride your scooter. What do you prefer?"

Without saying anything, she grabbed her scooter, and we all headed toward the park. There, her younger siblings rode their bikes on the paved path. Meanwhile our oldest was slowly riding her scooter with a frown. Then she got off her scooter, threw it fiercely to the ground, and sat down on the grass with her head curled up into her knees.

It felt tempting at this moment to say, "Please don't throw your scooter!" As parents, it can feel very difficult when the toys we work hard to provide for our kids are not treated with care. However, we recognized that our child was having a hard time and feeling upset. As she sat with her face planted in her knees, I (Neddy) approached her and sat down quietly beside her.

"It feels hard to wait to get a new bike," our daughter said.

I was impressed by her willingness to share what she was feeling. "It is hard to wait," I replied. And I continued to sit next to her as her younger siblings rode their bikes with laughter and large smiles on their faces.

After a couple of minutes, our oldest took a deep sigh and relaxed her body. She stood up, and leaving her scooter on the ground, she grabbed her soccer ball instead and started kicking it on the grass.

It didn't necessarily look like dancing, but in its simplicity, this interaction demonstrates the power of pausing, naming and honoring one's experience, and then responding spontaneously with creativity. For us, this is what dancing is all about. Our daughter was able to acknowledge what she was feeling, and when she felt accompanied in her experience, she was able to play again, this time with something new. Her ability to grab her soccer ball and discover a new way to play was an embodied practice of celebrating the gift of being truly alive.

On the surface, it may seem like our children's emotions are intense and constantly moving like waves in an ocean. However, deep within our children lies inner wisdom and a natural longing to be loved. We share this longing within ourselves, too. We have the opportunity to accompany our children in their experience and empower them to tap into their deeper wells of wisdom and creativity. At the park, our daughter was able to pause, take a deep breath, become self-aware, and respond because of the practices we had instilled in her over time. These kinds of moments do not always happen when something feels hard. However, with practice, taking time to pause, breathe, self-reflect, and respond with love and creativity becomes more and more natural for everyone in the home. Embrace this as a practice, and when you feel you have made a mistake or acted in a way you regret, go back to your practice. It is never too late to pause, reflect, restore with love, and create something new.

All children are uniquely gifted by the Divine. As parents, it is our task to support our children as they discover their innate gifts. In her book *Braiding Sweetgrass*, botanist Robin Wall Kimmerer shares that the Indigenous perspective is that an educated person is not the person who earns academic degrees, but rather the person who knows their gift and offers it to the world for the sake of the world.[3] We believe this insight is transformative and valuable because it aligns with the reality that all of our lives are interconnected. When we offer our gifts to the world with love, all of life flourishes. Remind your child daily that they have valuable gifts to offer and pray for discernment on how to identify your child's gifts. Some of the gifts we notice in our children are physical strength, drawing abilities, empathy, thoughtfulness, creative imagination, gentleness, contagious joy . . . There are so many gifts our children offer, and when we help them notice these gifts and how they bless our home, our children feel more empowered to live into the truest version of themselves.

Of course, dancing can and should mean dancing, too. We love to invite each of our children to choose a song, and we literally have a family dance party at home. Dance is one of the most accessible contemplative practices for children, and they often love to do it whenever music is playing. Dancing freely is incredibly liberating. It is a powerful way for our bodies and our children's bodies to shake off the burden of shame or bondage and freely move and create with Christ. If, as children, we felt that we were not given space or time to dance or move freely, as parents we now have the ability to give our inner child permission to dance and be free!

Other ways to practice dance

Drawing a parts map

As noted, all you need for this activity is paper and coloring supplies. On your paper draw a large heart or draw an outline of a human body; either will work fine. Next, begin to notice what emotions or parts of you are activated. Choose any color crayon you desire and begin to color in the heart (or body) where the emotion or activated part of you is taking up space. Use different colors to represent each feeling or part of you that is showing up. Once you have colored your different parts, observe and share what you notice. What colors did you choose? Where in the heart or body does the emotion or part of you show up? Be open to whatever insights might emerge.

If your child practices this with you, offer them gratitude for sharing in this practice together. Drawing a parts map has been a huge support to our children as they process big feelings in a creative and more grounded way.

Freely dance

At the end of the day, it can be incredibly helpful to create some space with your children for dancing. You can ask them what song they would like to dance to and if they do not offer a suggestion, then you can choose a song. As the song plays, there are no requirements except to allow your body to dance and move as it desires. If your child does not want to engage, that is okay. Your example powerfully models to them the liberating power of moving our bodies in a way that helps us reconnect to ourselves. Dancing literally frees our bodies from carrying heavy burdens and helps us feel lighter and renewed as we prepare to rest. When you are done dancing, offer them the question, "How does your body feel after dancing?" Validate and affirm their experience.

Dance with nature

Find some time to be outside in an environment with grass, trees, and plants. Then, experiment with the following activities with your child or children.

If possible, invite your children to join you in being barefoot on the grass. Notice what the ground feels like on your skin and acknowledge the support of Earth's gravity as it holds your body. Ask your children what the grass feels like to them. Invite them to use their imagination and ask them what they imagine is happening in the grass. What animals live there and what are they doing? You can also encourage dancing on the grass if they are able to. Invite your children to freely dance with bare feet on the ground. After taking time to dance, ask your children how they and their bodies are feeling, and affirm their experience.

If there is a slight breeze or wind, invite your children to notice how the tree branches and leaves sway in the wind. We learned from a Buddhist teacher to call these "dancing trees." Invite your child to imagine that they are tree branches and to move their body like the dancing trees. Join them in this practice and notice what this brings up for you. Also, ask your children how this practice makes them feel.

BORED practice

Our sister-in-law is a former elementary school teacher. She taught us how to offer our young children options when they feel bored using an acronym for ways to discover something new. Feel free to create new words for each letter of the acronym if you feel so inspired!

Remember, when you use your imagination, it not only models to your child how to be imaginative, but it sparks your child to tap into their own imaginative abilities.

Build:	Build something new with blocks, magnet tiles, or craft supplies. Allow your imagination to be free.
Outside:	Play outside or go on a walk.
Read or rest:	Read a book or cuddle a stuffed animal as you lay down for rest.
Exercise:	Engage in a sport or exercise routine.
Draw or dance:	Draw, color, or turn on some music and dance!

Conclusion

Transforming the World One Act at a Time

And now faith, hope, and love remain. . . .
—1 Corinthians 13:13

The call to sacred parenthood requires a radical shift in our hearts and minds. We agree with the apostle Paul's words in 1 Corinthians 13 that three realities remain in our lives as Christians, and they are *faith*, *hope*, and *love*. We would like to offer our own translation of these three characteristics and show how cultivating them enables parenthood to transform us.

We see faith not as a dogmatic belief but rather as the ongoing openness to face life as it is. Faith is not about changing things to fit our image. It is about being changed by each moment through openness to God's mysterious work. True faith requires belief in oneself (as a participant in all of reality) as well as belief that there is indeed a harmonious rhythm at the core of all things. Faith calls us to realize the fullness of our lives through our actions. As Christians, we believe that it is our faith that makes us well—and whole (Mark 10:52).

When it comes to hope, we see this as confidence. Our confidence is not in set outcomes or in the fact that things will always work out or be easy. In fact, life often confronts us with the most horrific realities. Instead, hope is the awareness that something is happening at the depths of life (and mostly invisible but discernible) that is at work to renew and re-create each moment so that love may be deepened and expanded. Hope is lived out when we act in ways that include but still go far beyond each of our lives or what we will see during our lifetime. Hope is then both experienced in the present and it is connected to the eternal. Hope is what keeps the Earth going even after five mass extinctions on our planet.[1] And hope is the very confidence at the core of reality that enables us to act courageously in the present moment to address suffering in all forms. It is hope that allows us to speak the truth, be bold, and make amends when necessary.

Lastly, love is considered the "greatest" because it is this movement that withholds nothing but pours out one's life for the sake of the whole. Love calls us to honor our own personal lives as well as the lives of others as precious before God. For us, we look to the model of Jesus, who defined the greatness of love with the words "No one has greater love than this, to lay down one's life for one's friends" (John 15:13). In this powerful verse, Jesus calls us to at least two transformations. The first is the consciousness of friendship. Jesus challenges those listening to move beyond any "us/them" mentality and come to know all beings in life as "friends." It is this consciousness of friendship that allows Jesus to utter these words while he hangs on the cross: "Father, forgive them, for they do not know what they are doing" (Luke 23:34).

But it goes deeper. In Jesus' example, we see that love is not about just becoming a friend to the world, in all its waywardness, but a call to give oneself to that life so that all things can be holistically nourished. The *giving away* that Jesus models is not one that refuses to challenge injustice. Nor does it perpetuate abuse or violence to our lives in any form (we know in fact it was his challenging of injustice, including his turning of tables in the temple, that led to Jesus' death!). On the contrary, Jesus' act of giving away his own life does not discriminate but is all-inclusive. It is not an act of self-righteousness or pride but one of deep humility and interconnectedness with all life.

We also know Jesus' act of giving away was not without struggle. His prayer in the garden of Gethsemane on the night of his arrest reveals his desire for another way to be possible (Luke 22:42). But Jesus' giving away of his life is consistent with his teachings and lifestyle of nonviolence, which tells us that there are indeed times when we cannot avoid suffering, and we must be willing to accept this (if necessary) so that truth can be made manifest in our lives and the whole can be nourished. Jesus' love is a continuous *emptying* of himself (Philippians 2:7). Through this emptying, he is fully available for love to become transparent through him. Love is an act of emptying any desires that are less than total love for all because it is a willingness to be poured out for the sake of the whole.

Parenthood calls us to practice faith, hope, and love—or in our own translation, openness, confidence, and self-emptying. When we do, we will see that the world is further made into faith, hope, and love. We do not have to wait for tomorrow to practice this. We can turn to God and trust that infinite compassion is leading us toward this and will empower us to live this out when we make our requests known to God.

We have learned about these things in our household, especially on Sunday mornings. Every Sunday we begin our day with food together, and then we sing a few songs of praise. After this, we pray for each other and the world. We finish by reading a passage from a Bible storybook.[2] On one particular morning, we read a story from Matthew 4 where Jesus invites the fisherfolk he encounters with the words "Follow me." As we read, we animatedly acted out the story with the kids. At one point, Jesus says to the fishermen, "I will teach you to fish for people"—immediately sparking our children's curiosity.

"How big were the fish?" they exclaimed. "How do you fish a human?"

Our nine-year-old reflected more deeply and responded, "It means we don't just love ourselves. We work so we can give love to others."

In the tradition and lineage of Jesus, God's spirit in us calls us to fish for people—a call to love ourselves and others. Parenting can deeply root us in this calling, and we become fishers of all that is vulnerable inside and beyond us so that everyone can know how precious and loved they are by God. That morning with our children, we ended our time with a prayer: "Holy One, expand our capacity to love this world and all that is tender inside. Give us strength to love with fierce compassion, and to have the power of your love to be present in this world. Ground us in trust so that together we will create a world where all will flourish."

We believe none of this work will happen by ourselves. But we must be intentional about reaching out to one another, the Divine, and the world. We hope that this book encourages you to make that first contact with those around you, whether they are biologically related or chosen loved ones—grandparents, relatives, neighbors, or even friends—so that your household can rediscover the joy of being in community. Let us walk this road together and create the path to peace by walking in peace, one step at a time.

Acknowledgments

It is truly difficult to bring proper acknowledgment to all the wonderful beings who have accompanied us in our parenting journey. We first want to acknowledge the presence of the Divine, who lives in us and gives freely to all. The One who we know intimately and personally and has many names: Spirit, Love, Flow, Mystery, and Source. Our lives would not be possible without you. We give you thanks.

We thank our parents, who have taught us so much about what it means to live on purpose and for a purpose. Amos, Alma, Saúl, and Neddy, you have each walked your own paths of faith crossing cultural norms and have modeled for us courage in the storms of life. We are forever indebted to you for your leadership and prayers and the sacrifices you have made (and continue to make!) in our lives.

We honor the legacy of our grandparents, Joseph, Irene, Ricardo, Lusila, Zenaido, Angélica, Arturo, and Martha. You have granted us a lineage that places ultimate trust in God, and our prayer is to continue that example through all we do. We know your prayers have been heard, and that continues to guide us each day.

We give thanks to our beautiful and awe-inspiring children, Serenity, Valor, Río, and Kairo. You light up our world and continue to transform us into Love. Thank you for your presence, patience, humor, and laughter, as well as for calling us to divine accountability when our lives don't always match our words. Each time we look at you, we experience that which is beyond any description. It is the honor of a lifetime to be your parents.

We extend a big heartfelt thanks to our nanny, Elena Allen. Thank you for offering our children love and kindness at home when we were away writing, working, or traveling for ministry. You have been an angel to us from above.

We honor and thank Bishop Yvette A. Flunder, Mother Shirley Miller, and Pastor Ann Jefferson, who have been visionary pastors and spiritual guides to us. When we were not sure whether we would ever go back to ministry, your example confirmed to us there was a place for us. Your commitment to radical inclusion at every level has enriched our lives and our world benefits from your example. When we approached you about the Radically Inclusive Parenting Project, your response was a resounding yes! And since then, you have repeatedly told us, "I hope you feel the wind beneath your wings!" There is truly nothing like the spiritual cover you have given us which has helped us become all that we are. To God be the glory.

We thank the board of trustees at the Claremont School of Theology, Bishop Grant Hagiya, and Dean Andrew Dreitcer, who supported a leave in order to give us time to write this book. We also would be remiss not to mention the generosity of the Lilly Endowment for their financial support through their Christian Parenting and Caregiving Initiative, which has helped us find childcare support and gave us the material resources needed to promote radically inclusive parenting and caregiving.

Steps in the SACRED Practice

Our SACRED practice involves six movements. These movements can be practiced linearly, in the order that seems best in a given moment, or even individually. Each movement in the practice works together to support parenting as a path of *connecting to*, *being sustained by*, and allowing God to transform us. The SACRED practice is adaptive and intended to be engaged both individually and in community with others.

Settle: Settle into the presence of your sacred source

The first movement of the SACRED practice is to settle into the presence of your sacred source. Your sacred source could be God, the Spirit, the land, a natural element, or an ancestor. To begin, take an intentional pause and gently bring awareness to your breath. Then, position your body in a posture that feels both relaxed and aware. Allow yourself to breathe in a way that feels natural and right to you. Let each breath be a reminder that you are infinitely loved.

When thoughts of the past or future enter your mind, gently let each thought go and return to your breath. If you need more support, find a word or phrase you can return to as an anchor whenever you notice a thought arise. For example, you might choose the word "love." Gently say this word whenever you notice your mind wander. When you say your word, return your awareness back to your breath.

Say your grounding word or phrase as often as you need. The point isn't to stop thinking, but to commit to the practice of gently noticing your thoughts and returning back to the present moment.

Next, bring your awareness into your body. Notice where your body feels any tension, energy, or pain, and gently move your body in a way that feels right to you. You might turn your neck from side to side, gently roll your shoulders back, or roll out tension in your ankles. Trust your body to guide your movement.

Invite your sacred source to accompany you. Your sacred source could be God, the Spirit, the land, a natural element, or an ancestor. Identify which sacred source feels supportive to you in this moment. Continue to keep your awareness on your sacred source. You might visualize an image or recite a scripture or mantra that helps you experience the sacred presence. Settle into the sacred's presence just as you are with no agenda.

After a few minutes, whenever you feel ready, offer gratitude to your sacred source for accompanying you. Gently bring awareness back to your breath, then to your body, then to the physical space you are in.

End by offering gratitude to yourself for this gift of experiencing sacred stillness. If it feels right, you can place your hands on your heart, take a small bow, or place your hands on your lower abdomen as a sign of gratitude and honor for the sacred encounter.

There is no set time limit to this practice. If this is your first time experiencing stillness, you can try this practice for five minutes and then increase the number of minutes over time as you feel ready.

We encourage you to practice pausing and settling in at any point in the day whether it be for thirty minutes or thirty seconds. Whether you are alone in a quiet moment or surrounded by chaos, you can practice bringing your awareness to your breath and body and inviting your sacred source to accompany you.

Acknowledge: Notice and acknowledge thoughts, emotions, and bodily sensations

To begin, you are invited to find your inner grounding by connecting to your sacred source, as described in the previous movement.

Then, in a posture of stillness and receptivity, simply begin to notice what thoughts, emotions, or bodily sensations you are experiencing. Do not rush yourself. Simply notice what you are experiencing.

If you notice your mind getting distracted by thoughts about the past or future, simply bring awareness back to your breath, allowing your breath to be an anchor for you in the present moment. Gently let go of any inclination to judge yourself during this practice. Simply return to your breath and keep taking note.

As you notice what is coming up for you, is there a thought or thought pattern that comes to mind? Take notice of your thoughts and acknowledge them. If it feels right, you can say to the thought or thought pattern, "I see you, and I'm here."

Is there an emotion or multiple emotions that are surfacing? You can say to each emotion, "I see you, and I'm here."

What is your body experiencing? Any tension, pain, tightness, heat, coolness, tingling, or numbness? You can send loving compassion to the part of your body that is activated and move your body in any way that feels supportive. It might look like swaying side to side, placing your hands over your heart, gently rolling out your neck and shoulders, or stretching, for example.

To each part of you that is showing up, each thought, emotion, or bodily sensation, offer it loving acknowledgment by letting it know that you are here to bear loving witness to its experience. Again, you might say, "I see you, and I'm here."

When you feel ready, gently bring your awareness back to your breath, then your body, and then into the physical space you are in.

Take a final deep breath and offer gratitude to yourself and to the Divine for the gift of this experience.

This acknowledgment practice helps develop a greater capacity to be present in life as it is in Love. True love does not seek to impose an agenda but rather is present as life flows. When we practice noticing our real experience and can bear loving witness to it, we connect to the greater Source of Love in us who cares for us in all circumstances.

Curiosity: Listen to the stories of the parts within

Begin by inviting your sacred source to accompany you. Once you are in a grounded state, one that is calm, compassionate, and curious, notice what part of you (a thought, emotion, or bodily sensation) seems to carry the most energy and is drawing your attention the most. Note that if you do not feel curiosity, see if you can get curious first rather than pressing on.

When you have acknowledged a part of you that you want to explore more deeply and you are feeling curious about it, let this part of yourself know that you are willing to get to know it. You might ask this part of yourself, "If you could talk, what would you want to share? I'm here to listen."

Remain in a posture of stillness and receptivity, deeply listening to what this part of you is communicating. Does it have a story? Is there a memory associated with it? Where did it originate from? What beliefs or assumptions does it carry?

You can dialogue internally with that part of you, or if it helps, you can write out what information you are gathering from it.

When you feel that this part of you has finished sharing its story, ask it, "What are you longing for? And how can I support you?"

Remain openhearted and willing to listen to how this part of you is seeking your support and care. It might be wanting more time to rest, or more quality time with a loved one. It might be wanting you to take a risk, or to trust in your creative potential. Whatever it has to share, trust in its wisdom.

When you have finished listening to this part and the practice feels complete, offer it deep gratitude for its willingness to confide in you.

Restore: Ask your sacred source to reveal an invitation to restoration

Begin by inviting your sacred source to accompany you as you reflect on a recent or current challenging situation. Take your time as you deeply reflect on your challenging experience and notice what parts within yourself are activated.

Then, ask the Divine, or your sacred source, to reveal how you might restore right relationship with someone. Hold an inner posture of stillness as you wait and listen, noticing what the Divine might reveal to you.

Perhaps your invitation is to initiate an honest conversation with someone or to identify a boundary that is necessary for your well-being. Perhaps, it is to offer an apology to someone you hurt or to invite someone to share a meal with you. Perhaps your invitation is to offer yourself daily affirmations or to let go of something that no longer serves you. Perhaps, it is to reconnect with nature and spend more time caring for animals or plants. Trust in your inner wisdom, which flows from the Divine, and be open to receive your divine invitation to restoration.

When you feel the practice is complete, offer gratitude to your sacred source for lovingly accompanying you in this challenging experience.

This practice is an act of faith, trust that the Divine will reveal, at the right time, how to respond to your situation in love. Holding an inner posture of stillness does not require your body to be still. As you wait to hear from the Divine, you can maintain an inner posture of stillness as you walk, draw, hum, sing, write, or dance. Open your mind, heart, and body to hear and notice what is being revealed to you. Invite God to lead your response so that it is guided with love to yourself and to the situation.

Enjoy: Savor the newfound connection experienced in your loving response

Find a comfortable position where you can engage in self-reflection. Bring your awareness to your breath and allow yourself to simply be still for about a minute, anchoring your awareness in the natural rhythm of your breath.

Then, reflect on a recent memory when you experienced deep joy or restoration of relationship with yourself, God, or another. It could be a moment when you hugged a loved one or when you took time to offer yourself care. It could be when you experienced intimacy with God or the sacred. Notice which memory comes to mind, and for the next few minutes, allow yourself to sink deeper into this memory, remembering how each of your senses was engaged.

Allow the goodness of this experience to permeate your whole being. Give yourself permission to savor joy.

Then, notice if a word, color, or image comes to mind that feels connected to this experience of joy. The image could be a body of water, a plant, an animal, or anything that will help you remember this moment. Allow the word, color, or image to be a reminder to you of the joy you felt in this experience.

When you feel ready, take a few deep breaths to help you settle back into your body and gently bring your awareness back into your physical space.

Offer yourself gratitude for giving yourself the gift of savoring restorative connection and joy.

This movement is about further integrating new life into your body and personal experience. It is easy to move quickly from one thing to the next, but this practice is about allowing yourself to savor the richness of life. It is also helpful to imagine what concrete action you might take afterward to remind yourself of the gifts you have received in this moment. Perhaps you can create an image, ritual, candle lighting, or something else to tangibly anchor this experience in your spirit.

Dance: Celebrate deep transformation

Find a quiet space where you can reflect internally. Invite your sacred source to accompany you and take a few deep breaths to help you settle into the present moment.

Next, recall a recent moment when you experienced deep love and connection. Allow this memory to sink in for a few minutes remembering how your senses were activated in that experience.

Next, begin to imagine what celebration could look like as you honor the gifts granted to you in your life. What would it look like to deepen and expand the energy of those gifts you received, perhaps through a shared meal, creating art, building community, engaging in play, connecting with nature, singing a song, or offering a dance? Allow your imagination to flow freely. Notice what act of celebration feels most right to you.

Offer gratitude to your sacred source for the newfound aliveness you have experienced, and cherish the celebration!

Dance allows us to creatively act from a place of newfound, or restored, aliveness. It is a place of openness to the world as our actions flow out of a place of full-heartedness, generosity, and care. Dance is profoundly spontaneous and creative. We can dance—however it looks—without any expectation of a particular outcome. It is a pure overflow of one's experience and is the returning place for the SACRED practice to begin again, finding grounding and settling in the divine flow of reality.

Our Go-To Phrases for Family Life

Language is so powerful in family life. We continue to learn how to be more intentional with the words and language we use. We hope to foster a culture that promotes radical love and compassion in every aspect of our human experience. We have started to rely on some daily go-to phrases that we use at home to cultivate a spirit of connection, care, and compassion as a family. We trust that doing so will help our children believe in their own preciousness and be empowered to promote care and compassion for the sake of the entire world. We invite you to use (and adapt) them for your own household.

1. *Each of us matters in this family and we are here to support each other.* This phrase helps us remember to honor our individuation as well as our communal identity as a family. We want to practice respecting individual needs while also considering the needs of the whole. This is a delicate dance that is not always easy, however, with practice, we learn how to support one another in love and mutuality.

2. *We honor and respect our bodies and the bodies of others.* This phrase teaches our children to value their bodies as well as the bodies of others. It also helps our children learn that their holistic well-being is intimately connected to their bodily agency and well-being. We were inspired by Cindy Wang Brandt in her book *Parenting Forward* to teach our children to live with bodily agency and courage. Brandt offers in her book to teach your children to say, "My body is my body. It belongs to me."[1]

3. *Our bodies are a gift. Our bodies help us feel love.* We want to foster embodied awareness in our children so that they can value the skin they were born with and appreciate the gift of what their bodies can do for them.

4. *What does your body feel and need? It's good to listen to your body.* We say these words regularly at home to support our children as they cultivate more bodily presence and attunement. Dominant culture trains us to deny our body's wisdom. We hope to teach our children the value of being present to themselves and listening to their bodies.

5. *God loves you! And God lives in your heart, in your body, and in the whole world.* Our children hear these words daily as a reminder that they can never be separated from the love of God.

6. *God's love gives us the power to tell the truth.* This helps our children know that God's spirit has empowered them to embody love and truth in their community and in the world.

7. *You are loved just for being you.* This helps our children remember that they are infinitely loved just as they are and that they do not have to do anything to try to earn more love.

8. *I love you unconditionally. Even when it feels hard, my love is here to stay.* This helps our children learn that true love is constant and not dependent on circumstances. When we say this during a difficult moment, it reminds us that love is always with us to hold us and guide us. This teaches our children that we can experience love in all circumstances, happy, hard, and sad.

9. *True strength is found in how we love.* This teaches our children that strength is not defined by domination over others, but rather by the ability to love all others at all times.

10. *I am here to listen. I'm with you in this.* This helps our children learn what they have to say is valuable and important and they are not alone in their experiences. It also creates a culture of true listening and not suppressing or dismissing anyone's voice.

11. *What you feel is important. I'm here to support you.* This helps our children feel a sense of safety to share what they feel. They learn to see their emotions as important and something that offers valuable information on how to understand and connect to themselves.

12. *You are so creative. I love your creativity.* We foster creativity in our home and this phrase is used whenever any form of creativity is expressed. We value creative expression in our

home because it supports living out of a free and liberated heart. We believe God created us to be creative in the world.

13. *What ideas do you have?* This creates a culture where we choose to consider and listen to the ideas of others and collaborate on how to take next steps together.

14. *Thank you, God, for another day. Thank you, Sun, for rising again.* We say this every morning with our children, and we face in the direction of the sun as we offer our thanks. This practice helps us deepen the inner quality of gratitude and helps us begin our day with appreciation for the life we've been given.

15. *Thank you, Earth, for being our home and providing us with food, medicine, and beauty.* We also say this each morning to begin our day. This phrase helps us remember that our bodies are deeply connected to the Earth.

Notes

INTRODUCTION

1. Nereyda Yong and Aizaiah G. Yong, "Parenting at Home: Reimagining Pastoral Theology During a Global Pandemic," *Feminist Studies in Religion*, January 12, 2022, https://www.fsrinc.org/parenting-at-home-reimagining-pastoral-theology-during-a-global-pandemic/. We wrote about many of these experiences in a blog for the Feminist Studies of Religion blog entitled "Parenting at Home," which was the initial impetus for this book.
2. Elizabeth A. Johnson, *She Who Is: The Mystery of God in Feminist Theological Discourse* (The Crossroad Publishing Company, 1992), 179.
3. Jaya Ramesh and Priya Saaral, *Parenting at the Intersections: Raising Neurodivergent Children of Color* (Review Press, 2024), xx. We are grateful for resources like *Parenting at the Intersections*, which discusses how those of us committed to holistic flourishing and creating households of belonging must also include those from our communities who experience neurodivergence. This work, they write, must "disrupt our socialization and conditioning on what it means to be 'normal.'"
4. In some ways it feels impossible to adequately speak to all the influences who have made an impression on our journey, but we would like to name some of the contemplatives who have poured life into us and encouraged our contemplative path. Some of these we have met personally, and others have mentored us from afar: Richard Rohr, Raimon Panikkar, Gloria Anzaldúa, Ann Jefferson, Ronald Rolheiser, Javier Melloni, Ishmael Tetteh, Barbara Holmes, and James Finley. However, two of the most significant teachers and contemplative guides to us who we have studied with more intensely would be Frank Rogers Jr. and Wendy Farley. Both emphasize a contemporary approach to spiritual formation with deep commitments to social change and liberation.
5. Bernard McGinn, ed., *The Essential Writings of Christian Mysticism* (Modern Library, 2006), xiv.
6. Howard Thurman, *Jesus and the Disinherited* (Beacon Press, 1996), xi.
7. F. Forrester Church and Terrence J. Mulry, ed., *The Macmillan Book of Earliest Christian Hymns* (Macmillan, 1988).

8. Lara McKenzie, "Parenthood: Beyond Maternity and Paternity," *Feminist Anthropology* 3, no. 2 (November 2022): 299–306, https://doi.org/10.1002/fea2.12105.
9. Gabriel Scheidecker, "Parents, Caregivers, and Peers: Patterns of Complementarity in the Social World of Children in Rural Madagascar," *Current Anthropology* (2022), https://doi.org/10.17169/refubium-34249.
10. Ada María Isasi-Díaz, "Defining Our 'Proyecto Histórico.': 'Mujerista' Strategies for Liberation," *Journal of Feminist Studies in Religion* 9, no. 1/2 (1993): 17–28. Isasi-Díaz uses the term "kin-dom" as a way of subversively describing the Kingdom of God as a community of kin or relationships built on mutuality rather than authoritarian leadership.
11. See Luke 8:40–42, 49–56 for the full story of the healing of the daughter of Jairus.

CHAPTER 1

1. Peter A. Dunn, *Holistic Healing: Theories, Practices, and Social Change* (Canadian Scholars Press, 2019), 118–21. Dancing is resistance for Indigenous and Black people in the United States whose bodies were objectified by colonial settlers. Dancing continues to be an important practice of collective healing.
2. Mike Morrell, "Contemplative Prayer, Queer Theology, and Aroma of Beauty with Wendy Farley," *Mike Morrell*, January 26, 2022, https://mikemorrell.org/2022/01/contemplative-prayer-queer-theology-and-aroma-of-beauty-with-wendy-farley.

CHAPTER 2

1. Tricia Hersey, *Rest Is Resistance: A Manifesto* (Little, Brown Spark, 2022).
2. Lauren Cook, "The Danger of Hurried Child Syndrome," *Psychology Today*, August 10, 2024, https://www.psychologytoday.com/us/blog/decision-principles/202408/the-danger-of-hurried-child-syndrome. The term "hurried child syndrome" originated with psychologist David Elkind.
3. Brother Lawrence, *The Practice of the Presence of God* (Whitaker House, 1982).
4. Jon Kabat-Zinn and Myla Kabat-Zinn, *Everyday Blessings: The Inner Work of Mindful Parenting* (Hachette Books, 1998).
5. Christine Valters Paintner, *Breath Prayer: An Ancient Practice for the Everyday Sacred* (Broadleaf, 2021).
6. Our settling practice is an adaptation of centering prayer that worked for us initially as parents. For more information on centering prayer, we recommend Cynthia Bourgeault, *Centering Prayer and Inner Awakening* (Rowman & Littlefield, 2004).
7. Luke Healy, "Yes, They Can Guide You," *Integral Christian Network*, October 2, 2021, https://www.integralchristiannetwork.org/writings/2021/10/2/yes-they-can-guide-you.
8. Handwashing or bathing as spiritual practice for the home was introduced to us by Nubian Flunder at one of the Parent & Caregiver Support Spaces hosted by The Radically Inclusive Parenting Project.
9. Zen walking meditation is inspired by Escuela Salmos in Choachí, Colombia, under the guidance of Father Víctor Ricardo Moreno Holguín.
10. Currently, we are reading through—and highly recommend—a book from our publisher by Chrissie Muecke, Jasmin Pittman Morrell, and Teresa Kim Pecinovsky, *The Peace Table: A Storybook Bible* (Herald Press, 2023).

CHAPTER 3

1. Yvette Flunder, "Church Interlude II. Healing Oppression Sickness," in *Queer Christianities*, ed. Kathleen T. Talvacchia, Mark Larrimore, and Michael F. Pettinger (New York University Press, 2020), 115–24.
2. F. Forrester Church and Terrence J. Mulry, eds., *The Macmillan Book of Earliest Christian Hymns*, (Macmillan, 1988) 4, 20, 7.
3. Mallory E. Bowers and Rachel Yehuda, "Intergenerational Transmission of Stress in Humans," *Neuropsychopharmacology* 41, no. 1 (January 2016): 232–44, https://doi.org/10.1038/npp.2015.247.
4. Daniel J. Siegel, *The Developing Mind: Toward a Neurobiology of Interpersonal Experience* (Guilford Press, 1999).
5. Cynthia Bourgeault, *The Meaning of Mary Magdalene: Discovering the Woman at the Heart of Christianity* (Shambhala, 2010), 77.
6. Cynthia Bourgeault, *The Wisdom Jesus: Transforming Heart and Mind—A New Perspective on Christ and His Message* (Shambhala, 2008), 80–81.
7. Richard Rohr, *Falling Upward: A Spirituality for the Two Halves of Life*, 1st ed. (Jossey-Bass, 2011), 158.
8. Cole Arthur Riley, *This Here Flesh: Spirituality, Liberation, and the Stories That Make Us* (Convergent, 2022), 13.
9. See David Berceli, *The Revolutionary Trauma Release Process: Transcend Your Toughest Times* (Namaste, 2008), which speaks about how long-held trauma can be released through literally shaking one's body.
10. See David Steindl-Rast, *Gratefulness, the Heart of Prayer: An Approach to Life in Fullness* (Paulist Press, 1984).

CHAPTER 4

1. Steven M. Rosman, "Sense the Wonder: Children, Spirituality, and Kabbalah," in *Opening the Inner Gates: New Paths in Kabbalah and Psychology*, ed. Edward Hoffman (Shambhala, 1995), 80.
2. Craig L. Anderson, Dante D. Dixson, Maria Monroy, and Dacher Keltner, "Are Awe-Prone People More Curious? The Relationship between Dispositional Awe, Curiosity, and Academic Outcomes," *Journal of Personality* 88, no. 4 (August 2020): 762–79, https://doi.org/10.1111/jopy.12524.
3. Dacher Keltner, *Awe: The New Science of Everyday Wonder and How It Can Transform Your Life* (Penguin, 2023).
4. Richard C. Schwartz and Pam Krause, "Internal Family Systems (IFS) & Children and Adolescents," *IFS Institute*, accessed November 5, 2022, https://courses.ifs-institute.com/item/internal-family-systems-ifs-children-adolescents-47290.
5. Anne Lamott, *Plan B: Further Thoughts on Faith* (Riverhead Books, 2005), 256.
6. See, for example, Conscious Stories, "Dr. Shefali Tsabary Talks about Bedtime with Andrew Newman," YouTube video, October 15, 2016, https://www.youtube.com/watch?v=XPfPcsWN4dg.

CHAPTER 5

1. See Sylvia Duckworth's "Wheel of Power/Privilege" graphic, which helps to visualize this dynamic, https://sdpride.org/wp-content/uploads/2022/11/Wheel-of-Power-Privilege-Sylvia-Duckworth.pdf.

2. Daniel Thorson, "Waking Up in the Monster Factory Featuring Vinay Gupta," *Emerge: Making Sense of What's Next*, April 1, 2019, https://podcasters.spotify.com/pod/show/emerge/episodes/Vinay-Gupta---Waking-Up-in-the-Monster-Factory-pt--1-e3ikvk.
3. Raimundo Panikkar, *Myth, Faith, and Hermeneutics: Cross-Cultural Studies* (Paulist Press, 1980), 448.
4. Daniel Siegel and Ruth Buczynski, "Next Level Practitioner: Exploring the Roots of the Inner Critic," National Institute for the Clinical Application of Behavioral Medicine, https://s3.amazonaws.com/nicabm-stealthseminar/Next_Level_Practitioner/Week103/NEXT-Week103-Day5-CriticalInsights.pdf.
5. James Finley, "Finding Peace in a Troubled World," *Center for Action and Contemplation*, last modified December 1, 2021, https://cac.org/wp-content/uploads/2018/08/2018-08-Faculty-Reflection_James-Finley_unedited-transcript.pdf.
6. Frank Rogers Jr., *Practicing Compassion* (Upper Room, 2015).
7. Quoted in James Finley and Kirsten Oates, "Thomas Merton, Session 2," *Turning to the Mystics*, March 2020, https://cac.org/wp-content/uploads/2020/03/TTTM_Transcript_TMS2.pdf.
8. Many experts believe that the recent explosion of mental health challenges is correlated to the amount of screen time we allow in our lives. See, e.g., Jonathan Haidt, *The Anxious Generation: How the Great Rewiring of Childhood Is Causing an Epidemic of Mental Illness* (Penguin Press, 2024).
9. We were inspired to create this spiritual practice by listening to the teachings of African mystic Brother Ishmael Tetteh at his 2019 Mystical Explosion retreat in San Bernardino, California.
10. We give thanks and credit to Richard Elout for creating this tool, which we have used in our personal lives and as a way to parent more compassionately.

CHAPTER 6

1. Bstan-'dzin-rgya-mtsho, Desmond Tutu, and Doug Abrams, *The Book of Joy: Lasting Happiness in a Changing World* (Avery, 2016).
2. Augustine, *Confessions*, 1, 1,1.
3. Mario I. Águilar, *Church, Liberation and World Religions: Towards a Christian-Buddhist Dialogue*, Ecclesiological Investigations 14 (T & T Clark, 2012), 129.
4. Raimundo Panikkar, *Blessed Simplicity: The Monk as Universal Archetype* (Seabury Press, 1982), 30.
5. "The Examen," Loyola Marymount University, accessed September 19, 2024, https://mission.lmu.edu/centerformissionandidentity/ignatianway/ignatianresources/theexamen/.
6. See, for example, Brittany Rico, Paul Jacobs, and Alli Coritz, "2020 Census Shows Increase in Multiracial Population in All Age Categories," US Census Bureau, June 1, 2023, https://www.census.gov/library/stories/2023/06/nearly-a-third-reporting-two-or-more-races-under-18-in-2020.html.

CHAPTER 7

1. Eric Berne, "Transactional Analysis: A New and Effective Method of Group Therapy," *American Journal of Psychotherapy* 12, no. 4 (October 1958): 735–43.

2. Carmen Jimenez-Pride, *Focus on Feelings: Learning about My Feelings* (Play Therapy with Carmen, 2018).
3. Robin Wall Kimmerer, *Braiding Sweetgrass: Indigenous Wisdom, Scientific Knowledge and the Teachings of Plants* (Milkweed Editions, 2013).

CONCLUSION

1. Mirzam Abdurrachman Aswan and Yahdi Zaim, "5 Periods of Mass Extinction on Earth: Are We Entering the Sixth?," *The Conversation*, January 31, 2018, http://theconversation.com/5-periods-of-mass-extinction-on-earth-are-we-entering-the-sixth-57575.
2. As noted earlier, our current Bible storybook is *The Peace Table* by Chrissie Muecke, Jasmin Pittman Morrell, and Teresa Kim Pecinovsky (Herald Press, 2023).

OUR GO-TO PHRASES FOR FAMILY LIFE

1. Cindy Wang Brandt, *Parenting Forward: How to Raise Children with Justice, Mercy, and Kindness* (William B. Eerdmans, 2019), 39.

The Authors

Aizaiah G. Yong is a practical theologian, international educator, psychospiritual practitioner, ordained Pentecostal minister in the Christian Church (Disciples of Christ), and award-winning scholar. His books include *Multiracial Cosmotheandrism: A Practical Theology of Multiracial Experiences* (Orbis, 2023) and *Trauma and Renewal: Toward Spiritual, Communal, and Holistic Transformation* (Orbis, 2025). He currently serves as Associate Professor of Spirituality and Co-Director of the Center for Engaged Compassion at the Claremont School of Theology in Los Angeles, CA.

Nereyda Yong is an ordained minister in the Christian Church (Disciples of Christ) and spiritual director. Her passion is to support diverse families with resources that nurture a compassionate and just spirituality in their daily lives. She is the project director of the Radically Inclusive Parenting Project, an initiative of The Fellowship of Affirming Ministries. Nereyda has an MBA with a focus on business management as well as a Master of Divinity with a special emphasis in Christian Spirituality.

Nereyda and Aizaiah are the parents of four amazing and inspiring children.